63 crochet cable STITCHES

Do you love the old-world look of a cabled sweater?

Then why not crochet an afghan replete with the same rich, romantic patterns?

Sixty-three pattern stitches come together to create this heirloom-quality afghan. For the matching square pillow, simply assemble four of your favorite blocks for the front and create a single large block for the back. Or fashion a soft and elegant bolster pillow using sections of several pattern stitches.

This compendium of cable designs is only the latest volume in the Leisure Arts Easy-to-Crochet stitch library. Round out your pattern collection with Leisure Arts leaflet #555, *63 Easy-to-Crochet Pattern Stitches* and leaflet #2146, *63 More Easy-to-Crochet Pattern Stitches*. A world of touchable, crocheted texture awaits your discovery on every page!

LEISURE ARTS, INC.
Maumelle, Arkansas

1

lobster claw
CABLE

5

CABLED
checks

2

baby
CABLE

6

right twist 4 stitch
CABLE

3

three stitch
CABLE

7

left twist 4 stitch
CABLE

4

six stitch
CABLE

8

CABLED
eyelets

2

9
CABLED
diamonds

13
knotted
OVAL

10
LITTLE
diamonds

14
double entwined
CABLES

11
CABLE
in a diamond

15
LATTICE

12
plain 6 stitch
CABLE

16
triple twist
COLUMNS

3

17
triple
RIB

21
chained
CABLE

18
little
ROUNDS

22
chained
EIGHT

19
celtic
PLAIT

23
corded
RIB

20
open bobbled
CABLES

24
STAGHORI

25
alternating
CABLES

26
bobbled
CABLE
RIBS

27
twisted
COLUMNS

28
CABLED
rope

29 LOZENGE

30
triple
TWIST

31
broken
CROSS

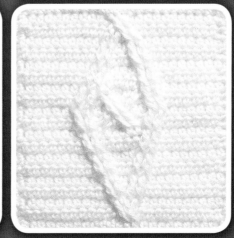

32
DIAMOND
X

5

33
copycat
CABLE

37
berry
TREE

34
twisted
DIAMONDS

38
round the
COLUMNS

35
chained
DIAMONDS

39
wheat
SHEAF

36
lattice
RIB

40
CABLED
bell

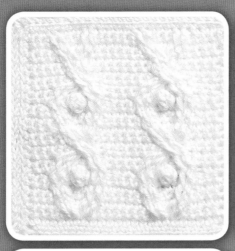

41
BOBBLED
rounds

45
roaming
CABLE

42
CABLED
bouquet

46
bobble
BRAID

43
CABLED
v's

47
bobbled
CHEVRONS

44
BLACK-
BERRIES

48
DOUBLE
waves & bobbles

7

49
TRIPLE
bobble chevrons

50
corded
DIAMOND

51
hollow
OAK

52
mini
**DIAMOND
RIB**

53
CABLED
hearts

54
drunken
CABLE

55
X'S & O'S

56
fancy
CHEVRON

8

57
triple
CORDED
CABLE

60 LANTERN

58
bobbled
WAVES

61
HONEY-
COMB

59
celtic
BORDER

62
wee
DIAMONDS

63
winter
BERRIES

afghan

Shown on front cover.

■■■□ INTERMEDIATE

Finished Size: 51" x 65" (129.5 cm x 165 cm)

MATERIALS
Medium Weight Yarn 🏷️4
   [3¹/₂ ounces, 166 yards
   (100 grams, 152 meters) per skein]:
    26 skeins
Crochet hooks, sizes G (4 mm) **and** H (5 mm)
   or sizes needed for gauge
Yarn needle

GAUGE: With larger size hook,
        each Square = 7" (18 cm)

AFGHAN

Make 63 Squares following instructions on pages 11-49.

Note: As you complete each Square, label it with its corresponding number for ease in placement at assembly.

FINISHING
EDGING
Change to smaller size hook.

Rnd 1: With **right** side facing, ch 1, (3 sc in corner, work 25 sc evenly spaced across to next corner) around; join with slip st to first sc, finish off: 112 sc.

ASSEMBLY
Afghan is assembled by joining 9 Squares into 7 vertical strips and then by joining strips.

Lay out Squares referring to the Assembly Diagram or in desired order.

Join Squares as follows:
With **wrong** sides together, top edge of first Square to bottom edge of second Square, and working through **inside** loops of **both** Squares, whipstitch Squares together *(Fig. 4, page 59)*.

Whipstitch strips together in same manner.

BORDER
Rnd 1: With **right** side facing and smaller size hook, join yarn with sc in center sc of top corner 3-sc group *(see Joining With Sc, page 59)*; sc in same st, ★ skip next sc, sc in next 26 sc, sc in next joining, (sc in next 27 sc, sc in next joining) across to last Square, sc in next 26 sc, skip next sc, 3 sc in center sc, skip next sc, sc in next 26 sc, sc in next joining, (sc in next 27 sc, sc in next joining) across to last Square, sc in next 26 sc, skip next sc; repeat from ★ once **more**, sc in same st as first sc; join with slip st to first sc: 896 sc.

To work Beginning Popcorn (uses one ch), ch 5, 5 sc in second ch from hook, drop loop from hook, insert hook in first sc of 5-sc group, hook dropped loop and draw through st. Ch 1 to close.

To work Popcorn (uses one ch), ch 2, 5 sc in second ch from hook, drop loop from hook, insert hook in first sc of 5-sc group, hook dropped loop and draw through st. Ch 1 to close.

Rnd 2: Work beginning Popcorn, dc in same st as beginning ch-5, skip next 3 sc, ★ (dc, work Popcorn, dc) in next sc, skip next 3 sc; repeat from ★ around; join with slip st to third ch of beginning ch-5, finish off.

ASSEMBLY DIAGRAM

42	21	7	8	5	2	18
27	62	51	6	50	28	31
33	9	4	15	29	24	22
32	30	23	37	14	17	19
16	25	26	41	55	1	56
44	43	39	34	54	36	46
38	45	59	35	49	60	20
10	58	3	40	12	47	48
57	53	63	11	61	52	13

lobster claw CABLE

Ch 25.

Row 1 (Right side)**:** Hdc in third ch from hook (2 skipped chs count as first hdc) and in each ch across: 24 hdc.

Note: Loop a short piece of yarn around any stitch to mark Row 1 as **right** side.

Row 2 AND ALL WRONG SIDE ROWS: Ch 2 (counts as first hdc, now and throughout), turn; hdc in next st and in each st across.

To work Front Post double crochet (abbreviated FPdc), YO, insert hook from **front** to **back** around post of st indicated *(Fig. 1, page 59)*, YO and pull up a loop even with st on hook, (YO and draw through 2 loops on hook) twice. Skip hdc **behind** FPdc.

Row 3: Ch 2, turn; hdc in next 2 hdc, † work FPdc around hdc one row **below** next hdc, hdc in next 6 hdc, work FPdc around hdc one row **below** next hdc †, hdc in next 2 hdc, repeat from † to † once, hdc in last 3 hdc.

Row 5: Ch 2, turn; hdc in next 3 hdc, ★ work FPdc around next FPdc, work FPdc around hdc one row **below** next hdc, hdc in next 2 hdc, skip next hdc, work FPdc around hdc one row **below** next hdc, work FPdc around next FPdc, hdc in next 4 hdc; repeat from ★ once **more**.

To work Front Post treble crochet (abbreviated FPtr), YO twice, insert hook from **front** to **back** around post of FPdc indicated *(Fig. 1, page 59)*, YO and pull up a loop, (YO and draw through 2 loops on hook) 3 times. Skip hdc **behind** FPtr.

Row 7: Ch 2, turn; hdc in next 4 hdc, † skip next 2 FPdc, work FPtr around next 2 FPdc, working in **front** of FPtr just made *(Fig. 3a, page 59)*, work FPtr around each skipped FPdc †, hdc in next 6 hdc, repeat from † to † once, hdc in last 5 hdc.

Repeat Rows 2-7 until piece measures 7" (18 cm) from beginning ch; do **not** finish off, mark last row as **bottom** edge.

Work Edging *(see Finishing, page 10)*.

baby CABLE

Ch 25.

Row 1 (Right side)**:** Hdc in third ch from hook (2 skipped chs count as first hdc) and in each ch across: 24 hdc.

Note: Loop a short piece of yarn around any stitch to mark Row 1 as **right** side.

Row 2: Ch 2 (counts as first hdc, now and throughout), turn; hdc in next hdc and in each hdc across.

To work Front Post double crochet (abbreviated FPdc), YO, insert hook from **front** to **back** around post of st indicated *(Fig. 1, page 59)*, YO and pull up a loop even with st on hook, (YO and draw through 2 loops on hook) twice. Skip hdc **behind** FPdc.

Row 3: Ch 2, turn; ★ hdc in next hdc, skip next hdc, work FPdc around hdc one row **below** next hdc, working in **front** of FPdc just made *(Fig. 3a, page 59)*, work FPdc around hdc one row **below** skipped hdc; repeat from ★ across to last 2 hdc, hdc in last 2 hdc.

Row 4: Ch 2, turn; hdc in next st and in each st across.

Row 5: Ch 2, turn; ★ hdc in next hdc, skip next FPdc, work FPdc around next FPdc, working in **front** of FPdc just made, work FPdc around skipped FPdc; repeat from ★ across to last 2 hdc, hdc in last 2 hdc.

Repeat Rows 4 and 5 until piece measures 7" (18 cm) from beginning ch; do **not** finish off, mark last row as **bottom** edge.

Work Edging *(see Finishing, page 10)*.

3 three stitch CABLE

Ch 25.

Row 1 (Right side)**:** Hdc in third ch from hook (**2 skipped chs count as first hdc**) and in each ch across: 24 hdc.

Note: Loop a short piece of yarn around any stitch to mark Row 1 as **right** side.

Row 2 AND ALL WRONG SIDE ROWS: Ch 2 (counts as first hdc, now and throughout), turn; hdc in next st and in each st across.

To work Front Post double crochet (abbreviated FPdc), YO, insert hook from **front** to **back** around post of st indicated (*Fig. 1, page 59*), YO and pull up a loop even with st on hook, (YO and draw through 2 loops on hook) twice. Skip hdc **behind** FPdc.

Row 3: Ch 2, turn; (hdc in next 2 hdc, work FPdc around hdc one row **below** next 3 hdc) across to last 3 hdc, hdc in last 3 hdc.

Row 5: Ch 2, turn; hdc in next 2 hdc, ★ † skip next FPdc, work FPdc around next 2 FPdc, working in **front** of FPdc just made (*Fig. 3a, page 59*), work FPdc around skipped FPdc †, hdc in next 2 hdc; repeat from ★ 2 times **more**, then repeat from † to † once, hdc in last 3 hdc.

Repeat Rows 2-5 until piece measures 7" (18 cm) from beginning ch; do **not** finish off, mark last row as **bottom** edge.

Work Edging (*see Finishing, page 10*).

4 six stitch CABLE

Ch 25.

Row 1 (Right side)**:** Hdc in third ch from hook (**2 skipped chs count as first hdc**) and in each ch across: 24 hdc.

Note: Loop a short piece of yarn around any stitch to mark Row 1 as **right** side.

Row 2 AND ALL WRONG SIDE ROWS: Ch 2 (counts as first hdc, now and throughout), turn; hdc in next st and in each st across.

To work Front Post treble crochet (abbreviated FPtr), YO twice, insert hook from **front** to **back** around post of st indicated (*Fig. 1, page 59*), YO and pull up a loop, (YO and draw through 2 loops on hook) 3 times. Skip hdc **behind** FPtr.

To work Front Post double crochet (abbreviated FPdc), YO, insert hook from **front** to **back** around post of st indicated (*Fig. 1, page 59*), YO and pull up a loop even with st on hook, (YO and draw through 2 loops on hook) twice. Skip hdc **behind** FPdc.

Row 3: Ch 2, turn; ★ † skip next 2 hdc, work FPtr around hdc one row **below** next 2 hdc, working in **front** of FPtr just made (*Fig. 3a, page 59*), work FPtr around hdc one row **below** each skipped hdc, work FPdc around hdc one row **below** next 2 hdc †, hdc in next 2 hdc; repeat from ★ once **more**, then repeat from † to † once, hdc in last hdc.

Row 5: Ch 2, turn; ★ † work FPdc around next 2 FPtr, skip next 2 FPtr, work FPtr around next 2 FPdc, working **behind** 2 FPtr just made (*Fig. 3b, page 59*), work FPtr around each skipped FPtr †, hdc in next 2 hdc; repeat from ★ once **more**, then repeat from † to † once, hdc in last hdc.

Row 7: Ch 2, turn; ★ † skip next 2 FPdc, work FPtr around next 2 FPtr, working in **front** of FPtr just made, work FPtr around each skipped FPdc, work FPdc around next 2 FPtr †, hdc in next 2 hdc; repeat from ★ once **more**, then repeat from † to † once, hdc in last hdc.

Repeat Rows 4-7 until piece measures 7" (18 cm) from beginning ch; do **not** finish off, mark last row as **bottom** edge.

Work Edging (*see Finishing, page 10*).

5 CABLED checks

Ch 25.

Row 1 (Right side)**:** Hdc in third ch from hook (**2 skipped chs count as first hdc**) and in each ch across: 24 hdc.

Note: Loop a short piece of yarn around any stitch to mark Row 1 as **right** side.

Row 2 AND ALL WRONG SIDE ROWS: Ch 2 (counts as first hdc, now and throughout), turn; hdc in next st and in each st across.

To work Front Post double crochet (abbreviated FPdc), YO, insert hook from **front** to **back** around post of st indicated (*Fig. 1, page 59*), YO and pull up a loop even with st on hook, (YO and draw through 2 loops on hook) twice. Skip hdc **behind** FPdc.

Row 3: Ch 2, turn; hdc in next hdc, ★ † skip next 2 hdc, work FPdc around hdc one row **below** next 2 hdc, working in **front** of FPdc just made (*Fig. 3a, page 59*), work FPdc around hdc one row **below** each skipped hdc †, hdc in next 4 hdc; repeat from ★ once **more**, then repeat from † to † once, hdc in last 2 hdc.

Row 5: Ch 2, turn; hdc in next hdc, work FPdc around next 4 FPdc, (hdc in next 4 hdc, work FPdc around next 4 FPdc) twice, hdc in last 2 hdc.

Row 7: Ch 2, turn; hdc in next hdc, ★ † skip next 2 FPdc, work FPdc around next 2 FPdc, working in **front** of FPdc just made, work FPdc around each skipped FPdc †, hdc in next 4 hdc; repeat from ★ once **more**, then repeat from † to † once, hdc in last 2 hdc.

Row 9: Ch 2, turn; hdc in next 5 hdc, † skip next 2 hdc, work FPdc around hdc one row **below** next 2 hdc, working in **front** of FPdc just made, work FPdc around hdc one row **below** each skipped hdc †, hdc in next 4 hdc, repeat from † to † once, hdc in last 6 hdc.

Row 11: Ch 2, turn; hdc in next 5 hdc, work FPdc around next 4 FPdc, hdc in next 4 hdc, work FPdc around next 4 FPdc, hdc in last 6 hdc.

Row 13: Ch 2, turn; hdc in next 5 hdc, † skip next 2 FPdc, work FPdc around next 2 FPdc, working in **front** of FPdc just made, work FPdc around each skipped FPdc †, hdc in next 4 hdc, repeat from † to † once, hdc in last 6 hdc.

Rows 14-19: Repeat Rows 2-7; do **not** finish off, mark last row as **bottom** edge.

Work Edging (*see Finishing, page 10*).

6 right twist 4 stitch CABLE

Ch 25.

Row 1 (Right side)**:** Hdc in third ch from hook (**2 skipped chs count as first hdc**) and in each ch across: 24 hdc.

Note: Loop a short piece of yarn around any stitch to mark Row 1 as **right** side and **bottom** edge.

Row 2 AND ALL WRONG SIDE ROWS: Ch 2 (counts as first hdc, now and throughout), turn; hdc in next st and in each st across.

To work Front Post double crochet (abbreviated FPdc), YO, insert hook from **front** to **back** around post of st indicated (*Fig. 1, page 59*), YO and pull up a loop even with st on hook, (YO and draw through 2 loops on hook) twice. Skip hdc **behind** FPdc.

Row 3: Ch 2, turn; hdc in next 2 hdc, ★ skip next 2 hdc, work FPdc around st one row **below** next 2 hdc, working **behind** FPdc just made (*Fig. 3b, page 59*), work FPdc around st one row **below** each skipped hdc, hdc in next 3 hdc; repeat from ★ 2 times **more**.

Row 5: Ch 2, turn; hdc in next 2 hdc, (work FPdc around next 4 FPdc, hdc in next 3 hdc) 3 times.

Repeat Rows 2-5 until piece measures 7" (18 cm) from beginning ch; do **not** finish off.

Work Edging (*see Finishing, page 10*).

left twist 4 stitch CABLE

Ch 25.

Row 1 (Right side)**:** Hdc in third ch from hook **(2 skipped chs count as first hdc)** and in each ch across: 24 hdc.

Note: Loop a short piece of yarn around any stitch to mark Row 1 as **right** side and **bottom** edge.

Row 2 AND ALL WRONG SIDE ROWS: Ch 2 (counts as first hdc, now and throughout), turn; hdc in next st and in each st across.

To work Front Post double crochet (abbreviated FPdc), YO, insert hook from **front** to **back** around post of st indicated (*Fig. 1, page 59*), YO and pull up a loop even with st on hook, (YO and draw through 2 loops on hook) twice. Skip hdc **behind** FPdc.

Row 3: Ch 2, turn; hdc in next 2 hdc, ★ skip next 2 hdc, work FPdc around st one row **below** next 2 hdc, working in **front** of FPdc just made (*Fig. 3a, page 59*), work FPdc around st one row **below** each skipped hdc, hdc in next 3 hdc; repeat from ★ 2 times **more.**

Row 5: Ch 2, turn; hdc in next 2 hdc, (work FPdc around next 4 FPdc, hdc in next 3 hdc) 3 times.

Repeat Rows 2-5 until piece measures 7" (18 cm) from beginning ch; do **not** finish off.

Work Edging (*see Finishing, page 10*).

CABLED eyelets

Ch 29.

Row 1 (Right side)**:** Sc in second ch from hook, ch 1, ★ skip next ch, sc in next 4 chs, ch 1; repeat from ★ across to last 2 chs, skip next ch, sc in last ch: 22 sc and 6 chs.

Note: Loop a short piece of yarn around any stitch to mark Row 1 as **right** side and **bottom** edge.

Row 2: Ch 1, turn; sc in each st and in each ch across.

To work Front Post treble crochet (abbreviated FPtr), YO twice, insert hook from **front** to **back** around post of st indicated (*Fig. 1, page 59*), YO and pull up a loop, (YO and draw through 2 loops on hook) 3 times. Skip sc **behind** FPtr.

Row 3: Ch 1, turn; sc in first sc, working **around** next sc (*Fig. 2, page 59*), dc in ch-1 sp one row **below** next sc, ★ skip first 3 sc of next 4-sc group, work FPtr around next sc, sc in next 2 sc, working in **front** of FPtr just made (*Fig. 3a, page 59*), work FPtr around first skipped sc, working **around** next sc, dc in ch-1 sp one row **below**; repeat from ★ across to last sc, sc in last sc.

Row 4: Ch 1, turn; sc in first 3 sts, ★ ch 2, skip next 2 sc, sc in next 3 sts; repeat from ★ across.

To work Front Post double crochet (abbreviated FPdc), YO, insert hook from **front** to **back** around post of st indicated (*Fig. 1, page 59*), YO and pull up a loop, (YO and draw through 2 loops on hook) twice. Skip st **behind** FPdc.

Row 5: Ch 1, turn; sc in first sc, work FPdc around st one row **below** next sc, ★ work FPtr around next FPtr, ch 2, work FPtr around next FPtr, work FPdc around st one row **below** next sc; repeat from ★ across to last sc, sc in last sc.

Row 6: Ch 1, turn; sc in next 3 sts, ★ ch 2, skip next ch-2 sp, sc in next 3 sts; repeat from ★ across.

Row 7: Ch 1, turn; sc in first sc, work FPdc around next FPdc, ★ skip next FPtr, work FPtr around next FPtr, working **behind** FPtr just made (*Fig. 3b, page 59*) and **around** ch-2 on previous 2 rows, 2 sc in ch-2 sp 2 rows **below** next ch-2, working in **front** of last FPtr made, work FPtr around skipped FPtr, work FPdc around next FPdc; repeat from ★ across to last sc, sc in last sc.

Row 8: Ch 1, turn; sc in first 3 sts, ★ ch 2, skip next 2 sc, sc in next 3 sts; repeat from ★ across.

Repeat Rows 5-8 until piece measures 7" (18 cm) from beginning ch; do **not** finish off.

Work Edging (*see Finishing, page 10*).

9 CABLED diamonds

Ch 27.

Row 1 (Right side)**:** Sc in second ch from hook and in each ch across: 26 sc.

Note: Loop a short piece of yarn around any stitch to mark Row 1 as **right** side and **bottom** edge.

Row 2 AND ALL WRONG SIDE ROWS: Ch 1, turn; sc in each st across.

To work Front Post double crochet (abbreviated FPdc), YO, insert hook from **front** to **back** around post of st indicated *(Fig. 1, page 59)*, YO and pull up a loop, (YO and draw through 2 loops on hook) twice. Skip sc **behind** FPdc.

Row 3: Ch 1, turn; sc in first sc, ★ † skip next 2 sc, work FPdc around sc one row **below** next 2 sc, working in **front** of FPdc just made *(Fig. 3a, page 59)*, work FPdc around sc one row **below** 2 skipped sc †, sc in next 6 sc; repeat from ★ once **more**, then repeat from † to † once, sc in last sc.

Row 5: Ch 1, turn; sc in first sc, work FPdc around next 4 FPdc, (sc in next 6 sc, work FPdc around next 4 FPdc) twice, sc in last sc.

Row 7: Ch 1, turn; sc in first sc, ★ † skip next 2 FPdc, work FPdc around next 2 FPdc, working in **front** of FPdc just made, work FPdc around each skipped FPdc †, sc in next 6 sc; repeat from ★ once **more**, then repeat from † to † once, sc in last sc.

Row 9: Ch 1, turn; sc in first 4 sc, skip first 2 FPdc, † work FPdc around next 2 FPdc, sc in next 4 sc, work FPdc around next 2 FPdc †, sc in next 2 sc, repeat from † to † once, sc in last 4 sc.

Row 11: Ch 1, turn; sc in first 5 sc, † work FPdc around next 2 FPdc, sc in next 2 sc, work FPdc around next 2 FPdc †, sc in next 4 sc, repeat from † to † once, sc in last 5 sc.

Row 13: Ch 1, turn; sc in first 6 sc, ★ skip next 2 FPdc, work FPdc around next 2 FPdc, working in **front** of FPdc just made, work FPdc around each skipped FPdc, sc in next 6 sc; repeat from ★ once **more**.

Row 15: Ch 1, turn; sc in first 6 sc, (work FPdc around next 4 FPdc, sc in next 6 sc) twice.

Row 17: Ch 1, turn; sc in first 6 sc, ★ skip next 2 FPdc, work FPdc around next 2 FPdc, working in **front** of FPdc just made, work FPdc around each skipped FPdc, sc in next 6 sc; repeat from ★ once **more**.

Row 19: Ch 1, turn; sc in first 5 sc, † work FPdc around next 2 FPdc, sc in next 2 sc, work FPdc around next 2 FPdc †, sc in next 4 sc, repeat from † to † once, sc in last 5 sc.

Row 21: Ch 1, turn; sc in first 4 sc, † work FPdc around next 2 FPdc, sc in next 4 sc, work FPdc around next 2 FPdc †, sc in next 2 sc, repeat from † to † once, sc in last 4 sc.

Row 23: Ch 1, turn; sc in first 3 sc, work FPdc around next 2 FPdc, sc in next 6 sc, work FPdc around next 4 FPdc, sc in next 6 sc, work FPdc around next 2 FPdc, sc in last 3 sc.

Row 25: Ch 1, turn; sc in first sc, work FPdc around next 2 FPdc, working in **front** of FPdc just made, work FPdc around second and third sc on Row 23, sc in next 6 sc, skip next 2 FPdc, work FPdc around next 2 FPdc, working in **front** of FPdc just made, work FPdc around each skipped FPdc, sc in next 6 dc, skip next 2 FPdc, work FPdc around next 2 sc on Row 23, working in **front** of FPdc just made, work FPdc around each skipped FPdc, sc in last sc.

Row 27: Ch 1, turn; sc in first sc, work FPdc around next 4 FPdc, (sc in next 6 sc, work FPdc around next 4 FPdc) twice, sc in last sc.

Row 29: Ch 1, turn; sc in first sc, ★ † skip next 2 FPdc, work FPdc around next 2 FPdc, working in **front** of FPdc just made, work FPdc around each skipped FPdc †, sc in next 6 sc; repeat from ★ once **more**, then repeat from † to † once, sc in last sc; do **not** finish off.

Work Edging *(see Finishing, page 10)*.

10 LITTLE diamonds

Ch 28.

Row 1 (Right side)**:** Hdc in third ch from hook (2 skipped chs count as first hdc) and in each ch across: 27 hdc.

Note: Loop a short piece of yarn around any stitch to mark Row 1 as **right** side.

Row 2 AND ALL WRONG SIDE ROWS: Ch 2 (counts as first hdc, now and throughout), turn; hdc in next st and in each st across.

To work Front Post double crochet (abbreviated FPdc), YO, insert hook from **front** to **back** around post of st indicated (*Fig. 1, page 59*), YO and pull up a loop even with st on hook, (YO and draw through 2 loops on hook) twice. Skip hdc **behind** FPdc.

To work Cluster, YO, insert hook from **front** to **back** around post of same st as last FPdc **or** around last leg of last Cluster made (*Fig. 1, page 59*), YO and pull up a loop, YO and draw through 2 loops on hook, YO, skip next 3 hdc, insert hook from **front** to **back** around post of st one row **below** next hdc, YO and pull up a loop, YO and draw through 2 loops on hook, YO and draw through 3 loops on hook. Skip st **behind** Cluster.

Row 3: Ch 2, turn; skip next 2 hdc, work FPdc around st one row **below** next hdc, hdc in next 3 hdc, (work Cluster, hdc in next 3 hdc) across to last 2 hdc, work FPdc around same st as last leg of Cluster made, hdc in last hdc.

Row 5: Ch 2, turn; hdc in next 2 hdc, (work Cluster, hdc in next 3 hdc) across.

Repeat Rows 2-5 until piece measures 7" (18 cm) from beginning ch; do **not** finish off, mark last row as **bottom** edge.

Work Edging (*see Finishing, page 10*).

11 CABLE in a diamond

Ch 27.

Row 1 (Right side)**:** Sc in second ch from hook and in each ch across: 26 sc.

Note: Loop a short piece of yarn around any stitch to mark Row 1 as **right** side and **bottom** edge.

Row 2 AND ALL WRONG SIDE ROWS: Ch 1, turn; sc in each st across.

To work Front Post double crochet (abbreviated FPdc), YO, insert hook from **front** to **back** around post of st indicated (*Fig. 1, page 59*), YO and pull up a loop, (YO and draw through 2 loops on hook) twice. Skip sc **behind** FPdc.

Row 3: Ch 1, turn; sc in first 12 sc, skip next sc, work FPdc around sc one row **below** next sc, working in **front** of FPdc just made (*Fig. 3a, page 59*), work FPdc around sc one row **below** skipped sc, sc in last 12 sc.

Row 5: Ch 1, turn; sc in first 11 sc, work FPdc around next FPdc, sc in next 2 sc, work FPdc around next FPdc, sc in last 11 sc.

Row 7: Ch 1, turn; sc in first 10 sc, work FPdc around next FPdc, sc in next sc, skip next sc, work FPdc around sc one row **below** next sc, working in **front** of FPdc just made, work FPdc around sc one row **below** skipped sc, sc in next sc, work FPdc around next FPdc, sc in last 10 sc.

Row 9: Ch 1, turn; sc in first 9 sc, work FPdc around next FPdc, sc in next 2 sc, skip next FPdc, work FPdc around next FPdc, working in **front** of FPdc just made, work FPdc around skipped FPdc, sc in next 2 sc, work FPdc around next FPdc, sc in last 9 sc.

Row 11: Ch 1, turn; sc in first 8 sc, work FPdc around next FPdc, sc in next 3 sc, skip next FPdc, work FPdc around next FPdc, working in **front** of FPdc just made, work FPdc around skipped FPdc, sc in next 3 sc, work FPdc around next FPdc, sc in last 8 sc.

Row 13: Ch 1, turn; sc in first 7 sc, work FPdc around next FPdc, sc in next 4 sc, skip next FPdc, work FPdc around next FPdc, working in **front** of FPdc just made, work FPdc around skipped FPdc, sc in next 4 sc, work FPdc around next FPdc, sc in last 7 sc.

Row 15: Ch 1, turn; sc in first 6 sc, work FPdc around next FPdc, sc in next 5 sc, skip next FPdc, work FPdc around next FPdc, working in **front** of FPdc just made, work FPdc around skipped FPdc, sc in next 5 sc, work FPdc around next FPdc, sc in last 6 sc.

Row 17: Ch 1, turn; sc in first 7 sc, work FPdc around next FPdc, sc in next 4 sc, skip next FPdc, work FPdc around next FPdc, working in **front** of FPdc just made, work FPdc around skipped FPdc, sc in next 4 sc, work FPdc around next FPdc, sc in last 7 sc.

Row 19: Ch 1, turn; sc in first 8 sc, work FPdc around next FPdc, sc in next 3 sc, skip next FPdc, work FPdc around next FPdc, working in **front** of FPdc just made, work FPdc around skipped FPdc, sc in next 3 sc, work FPdc around next FPdc, sc in last 8 sc.

Row 21: Ch 1, turn; sc in first 9 sc, work FPdc around next FPdc, sc in next 2 sc, skip next FPdc, work FPdc around next FPdc, working in **front** of FPdc just made, work FPdc around skipped FPdc, sc in next 2 sc, work FPdc around next FPdc, sc in last 9 sc.

Row 23: Ch 1, turn; sc in first 10 sc, work FPdc around next FPdc, sc in next sc, skip next FPdc, work FPdc around next FPdc, working in **front** of FPdc just made, work FPdc around skipped FPdc, sc in next sc, work FPdc around next FPdc, sc in last 10 sc.

Row 25: Ch 1, turn; sc in first 11 sc, work FPdc around next FPdc, skip next FPdc, work FPdc around next FPdc, working in **front** of FPdc just made, work FPdc around skipped FPdc, work FPdc around next FPdc, sc in last 11 sc.

Row 27: Ch 1, turn; sc in first 12 sc, work FPdc around next 2 FPdc, sc in last 12 sc.

Row 28: Ch 1, turn; sc in each st across.

Change to smaller size hook.

Edging: Ch 1, turn, work 3 sc in first sc, 2 sc in next sc, sc in next 10 sc, skip next FPdc, work FPdc around next FPdc, working in **front** of FPdc just made, work FPdc around skipped FPdc, sc in next 11 sc, 3 sc in next sc, work 25 sc evenly spaced across end of rows; working in free loops of beginning ch (*Fig. 5, page 59*), 3 sc in first ch, 2 sc in next sc, sc in next 23 chs, 3 sc in next ch, work 25 sc evenly spaced across end of rows; join with slip st to first sc, finish off: 112 sc.

12 plain 6 stitch CABLE

Ch 25.

Row 1 (Right side)**:** Hdc in third ch from hook (2 skipped chs count as first hdc) and in each ch across: 24 hdc.

Note: Loop a short piece of yarn around any stitch to mark Row 1 as **right** side and **bottom** edge.

Row 2 AND ALL WRONG SIDE ROWS: Ch 2 (counts as first hdc, now and throughout), turn; hdc in next st and in each st across.

To work Front Post treble crochet (abbreviated FPtr), YO twice, insert hook from **front** to **back** around post of st indicated (*Fig. 1, page 59*), YO and pull up a loop, (YO and draw through 2 loops on hook) 3 times. Skip hdc **behind** FPtr.

To work Front Post double crochet (abbreviated FPdc), YO, insert hook from **front** to **back** around post of st indicated (*Fig. 1, page 59*), YO and pull up a loop, (YO and draw through 2 loops on hook) twice. Skip sc **behind** FPdc.

Row 3: Ch 2, turn; hdc in next 3 hdc, ★ skip next 3 hdc, work FPtr around hdc one row **below** next 3 hdc, working in **front** of FPtr just made (*Fig. 3a, page 59*), work FPtr around hdc one row **below** each skipped hdc, hdc in next 4 hdc; repeat from ★ once **more**.

Row 5: Ch 2, turn; hdc in next 3 hdc, (work FPdc around next 6 FPtr, hdc in next 4 hdc) twice.

Row 7: Ch 2, turn; hdc in next 3 hdc, (work FPdc around next 6 FPdc, hdc in next 4 hdc) twice.

Row 9: Ch 2, turn; hdc in next 3 hdc, ★ skip next 3 FPdc, work FPtr around next 3 FPdc, working in **front** of FPtr just made, work FPtr around each skipped FPdc, hdc in next 4 hdc; repeat from ★ once **more**.

Repeat Rows 4-9 until piece measures 7" (18 cm) from beginning ch; do **not** finish off.

Work Edging (*see Finishing, page 10*).

13 KNOTTED OVAL

Ch 26.

Row 1 (Right side)**:** Hdc in third ch from hook (**2 skipped chs count as first hdc**) and in each ch across: 25 hdc.

Note: Loop a short piece of yarn around any stitch to mark Row 1 as **right** side and **bottom** edge.

Row 2 AND ALL WRONG SIDE ROWS: Ch 2 (counts as first hdc, now and throughout), turn; hdc in next hdc and in each st across.

To work Front Post double crochet (abbreviated FPdc), YO, insert hook from **front** to **back** around post of st indicated (*Fig. 1, page 59*), YO and pull up a loop even with st on hook, (YO and draw through 2 loops on hook) twice. Skip hdc **behind** FPdc.

Rows 3 and 5: Ch 2, turn; ★ hdc in next 2 hdc, work FPdc around st one row **below** next 2 hdc, hdc in next hdc, work FPdc around st one row **below** next 2 hdc; repeat from ★ 2 times **more**, hdc in last 3 hdc.

To work decrease (uses 4 FPdc), ★ YO, insert hook from **front** to **back** around post of **next** FPdc, YO and pull up a loop even with st on hook, YO and draw through 2 loops on hook; repeat from ★ 3 times **more**, YO and draw through all 5 loops on hook. Skip hdc **behind** decrease.

Row 7: Ch 2, turn; hdc in next 4 hdc, decrease, (hdc in next 6 hdc, decrease) twice, hdc in last 5 hdc.

To work Cluster (uses one st), ★ YO, insert hook from **front** to **back** around top of decrease, YO and pull up a loop even with st on hook, YO and draw through 2 loops on hook; repeat from ★ 3 times **more**, YO and draw through all 5 loops on hook. Skip hdc **behind** Cluster.

Row 9: Ch 2, turn; hdc in next 4 hdc, work Cluster, (hdc in next 6 hdc, work Cluster) twice, hdc in last 5 hdc.

Row 11: Ch 2, turn; ★ hdc in next 2 hdc, skip next hdc, work 2 FPdc around hdc one row **below** next hdc, hdc in next hdc, work 2 FPdc around hdc one row **below** next hdc; repeat from ★ 2 times **more**, hdc in last 3 hdc.

Rows 13 and 15: Ch 2, turn; ★ hdc in next 2 hdc, work FPdc around next 2 FPdc, hdc in next hdc, work FPdc around next 2 FPdc; repeat from ★ 2 times **more**, hdc in last 3 hdc.

Repeat Rows 6-13 until piece measures 7" (18 cm) from beginning ch; do **not** finish off.

Work Edging (*see Finishing, page 10*).

14 double entwined CABLES

Ch 25.

Row 1 (Right side)**:** Sc in second ch from hook and in each ch across: 24 sc.

Note: Loop a short piece of yarn around any stitch to mark Row 1 as **right** side and **bottom** edge.

Row 2 AND ALL WRONG SIDE ROWS: Ch 1, turn; sc in each st across.

To work Front Post double crochet (abbreviated FPdc), YO, insert hook from **front** to **back** around post of st indicated (*Fig. 1, page 59*), YO and pull up a loop, (YO and draw through 2 loops on hook) twice. Skip sc **behind** FPdc.

Row 3: Ch 1, turn; sc in first 7 sc, † skip next 2 sc, work FPdc around sc one row **below** next 2 sc, working in **front** of FPdc just made (*Fig. 3a, page 59*), work FPdc around sc one row **below** each skipped sc †, sc in next 2 sc, repeat from † to † once, sc in last 7 sc.

Row 5: Ch 1, turn; sc in first 7 sc, work FPdc around next 4 FPdc, sc in next 2 sc, work FPdc around next 4 FPdc, sc in last 7 sc.

Row 7: Ch 1, turn; sc in first 7 sc, † skip next 2 FPdc, work FPdc around next 2 FPdc, working in **front** of FPdc just made, work FPdc around each skipped FPdc †, sc in next 2 sc, repeat from † to † once, sc in last 7 sc.

Row 9: Ch 1, turn; sc in first 6 sc, work FPdc around next 2 FPdc, sc in next 2 sc, work FPdc around next 4 FPdc, sc in next 2 sc, work FPdc around next 2 FPdc, sc in last 6 sc.

Row 11: Ch 1, turn; sc in first 6 sc, work FPdc around next 2 FPdc, sc in next 2 sc, skip next 2 FPdc, work FPdc around next 2 FPdc, working in **front** of FPdc just made, work FPdc around each skipped FPdc, sc in next 2 sc, work FPdc around next 2 FPdc, sc in last 6 sc.

Rows 13-24: Repeat Rows 9-12, 3 times.

Row 25: Ch 1, turn; sc in first 7 sc, work FPdc around next 4 FPdc, sc in next 2 sc, work FPdc around next 4 FPdc, sc in last 7 sc.

Row 27: Ch 1, turn; sc in first 7 sc, † skip next 2 FPdc, work FPdc around next 2 FPdc, working in **front** of FPdc just made, work FPdc around each skipped FPdc †, sc in next 2 sc, repeat from † to † once **more**, sc in last 7 sc; do **not** finish off.

Work Edging (*see Finishing, page 10*).

15 LATTICE

Ch 27.

Row 1 (Right side)**:** Hdc in third ch from hook (2 skipped chs count as first hdc) and in each ch across: 26 hdc.

Note: Loop a short piece of yarn around any stitch to mark Row 1 as **right** side and **bottom** edge.

Row 2 AND ALL WRONG SIDE ROWS: Ch 2 (counts **as first hdc, now and throughout**), turn; hdc in next st and in each st across.

To work Front Post double crochet (abbreviated FPdc), YO, insert hook from **front** to **back** around post of st indicated (*Fig. 1, page 59*), YO and pull up a loop even with st on hook, (YO and draw through 2 loops on hook) twice. Skip hdc **behind** FPdc.

Row 3: Ch 2, turn; work FPdc around first 2 sts two rows **below**, hdc in next 8 hdc, skip next 2 hdc, work FPdc around hdc one row **below** next 2 hdc, working in **front** of FPdc just made (*Fig. 3a, page 59*), work FPdc around hdc one row **below** each skipped hdc, hdc in next 8 hdc, work FPdc around last 2 hdc two rows **below**, hdc in last hdc.

Row 5: Ch 2, turn; hdc in next hdc, ★ work FPdc around next 2 FPdc, hdc in next 6 hdc, work FPdc around next 2 FPdc, hdc in next 2 hdc; repeat from ★ once **more**.

Row 7: Ch 2, turn; hdc in next 2 hdc, work FPdc around next 2 FPdc, (hdc in next 4 hdc, work FPdc around next 2 FPdc) 3 times, hdc in last 3 hdc.

Row 9: Ch 2, turn; hdc in next 3 hdc, † work FPdc around next 2 FPdc, hdc in next 2 hdc, work FPdc around next 2 FPdc †, hdc in next 6 hdc, repeat from † to † once, hdc in last 4 hdc.

Row 11: Ch 2, turn; hdc in next 4 hdc, work FPdc around next 4 FPdc, hdc in next 8 hdc, work FPdc around next 4 FPdc, hdc in last 5 hdc.

Row 13: Ch 2, turn; hdc in next 4 hdc, † skip next 2 FPdc, work FPdc around next 2 FPdc, working in **front** of FPdc just made, work FPdc around each skipped FPdc †, hdc in next 8 hdc, repeat from † to † once, hdc in last 5 hdc.

Row 15: Repeat Row 9.

Row 17: Repeat Row 7.

Row 19: Repeat Row 5.

Row 21: Ch 2, turn; work FPdc around next 2 FPdc, hdc in next 8 hdc, work FPdc around next 4 FPdc, hdc in next 8 hdc, work FPdc around next 2 FPdc, hdc in last hdc.

Row 23: Ch 1, turn; work FPdc around first 2 FPdc, hdc in next 9 hdc, skip next 2 FPdc, work FPdc around next 2 FPdc, working in **front** of FPdc just made, work FPdc around each skipped FPdc, hdc in next 9 hdc, work FPdc around last 2 FPdc; do **not** finish off.

Work Edging (*see Finishing, page 10*).

triple twist
COLUMNS

Ch 25.

Row 1 (Right side)**:** Hdc in third ch from hook (**2 skipped chs count as first hdc**) and in each ch across: 24 hdc.

Note: Loop a short piece of yarn around any stitch to mark Row 1 as **right** side.

Row 2 AND ALL WRONG SIDE ROWS: Ch 2 (counts as first hdc, now and throughout), turn; hdc in next st and in each st across.

To work Front Post double crochet (abbreviated FPdc), YO, insert hook from **front** to **back** around post of st indicated (*Fig. 1, page 59*), YO and pull up a loop even with st on hook, (YO and draw through 2 loops on hook) twice. Skip hdc **behind** FPdc.

Row 3: Ch 2, turn; hdc in next 2 hdc, work FPdc around hdc one row **below** next 4 hdc, hdc in next 3 hdc, skip next 2 hdc, work FPdc around hdc one row **below** next 2 hdc, working in **front** of FPdc just made (*Fig. 3a, page 59*), work FPdc around hdc one row **below** each skipped hdc, hdc in next 3 hdc, work FPdc around hdc one row **below** next 4 hdc, hdc in next 3 hdc.

Rows 5 and 7: Ch 2, turn; hdc in next 2 hdc, work FPdc around next 4 FPdc, hdc in next 3 hdc, skip next 2 FPdc, work FPdc around next 2 FPdc, working in **front** of FPdc just made, work FPdc around each skipped FPdc, hdc in next 3 hdc, work FPdc around next 4 FPdc, hdc in last 3 hdc.

Rows 9, 11, and 13: Ch 2, turn; hdc in next 2 hdc, † skip next 2 FPdc, work FPdc around next 2 FPdc, working in **front** of FPdc just made, work FPdc around each skipped FPdc, hdc in next 3 hdc †, work FPdc around next 4 FPdc, hdc in next 3 hdc, repeat from † to † once.

Rows 15, 17, and 19: Ch 2, turn; hdc in next 2 hdc, work FPdc around next 4 FPdc, hdc in next 3 hdc, skip next 2 FPdc, work FPdc around next 2 FPdc, working in **front** of FPdc just made, work FPdc around each skipped FPdc, hdc in next 3 hdc, work FPdc around next 4 FPdc, hdc in last 3 hdc.

Do **not** finish off, mark last row as **bottom** edge.

Work Edging (*see Finishing, page 10*).

triple
RIB

Ch 25.

Row 1 (Right side)**:** Hdc in third ch from hook (**2 skipped chs count as first hdc**) and in each ch across: 24 hdc.

Note: Loop a short piece of yarn around any stitch to mark Row 1 as **right** side and **bottom** edge.

Row 2 AND ALL WRONG SIDE ROWS: Ch 2 (counts as first hdc, now and throughout), turn; hdc in next st and in each st across.

To work Front Post double crochet (abbreviated FPdc), YO, insert hook from **front** to **back** around post of st indicated (*Fig. 1, page 59*), YO and pull up a loop even with st on hook, (YO and draw through 2 loops on hook) twice. Skip hdc **behind** FPdc.

Row 3: Ch 2, turn; ★ hdc in next 2 hdc, work FPdc around hdc one row **below** next 3 hdc; repeat from ★ across to last 3 hdc, hdc in last 3 hdc.

Rows 5, 7, and 9: Ch 2, turn; ★ hdc in next 2 hdc, work FPdc around next 3 FPdc; repeat from ★ across to last 3 hdc, hdc in last 3 hdc.

Row 11: Ch 2, turn; ★ hdc in next 2 hdc, skip next 2 FPdc, work FPdc around next FPdc, working in **front** of FPdc just made (*Fig. 3a, page 59*), work FPdc around each skipped FPdc; repeat from ★ across to last 3 hdc, hdc in last 3 hdc.

Row 13: Ch 2, turn; ★ hdc in next 2 hdc, skip next FPdc, work FPdc around next 2 FPdc, working in **front** of FPdc just made, work FPdc around each skipped FPdc; repeat from ★ across to last 3 hdc, hdc in last 3 hdc.

Rows 15, 17, 19, and 21: Ch 2, turn; (hdc in next 2 hdc, work FPdc around next 3 FPdc) across to last 3 hdc, hdc in last 3 hdc; do **not** finish off.

Work Edging (*see Finishing, page 10*).

18 little ROUNDS

Ch 25.

Row 1 (Right side)**:** Sc in second ch from hook and in each ch across: 24 sc.

Note: Loop a short piece of yarn around any stitch to mark Row 1 as **right** side and **bottom** edge.

Row 2 AND ALL WRONG SIDE ROWS: Ch 1, turn; sc in each st across.

To work Front Post double crochet (abbreviated FPdc), YO, insert hook from **front** to **back** around post of st indicated (*Fig. 1, page 59*), YO and pull up a loop, (YO and draw through 2 loops on hook) twice. Skip sc **behind** FPdc.

Row 3: Ch 1, turn; sc in first 4 sc, work FPdc around sc one row **below** next 4 sc, sc in next 8 sc, work FPdc around sc one row **below** next 4 sc, sc in last 4 sc.

Row 5: Ch 1, turn; sc in first 2 sc, work FPdc around next 2 FPdc, (sc in next 4 sc, work FPdc around next 2 FPdc) 3 times, sc in last 2 sc.

Row 7: Ch 1, turn; sc in first sc, † work FPdc around next 2 FPdc, sc in next 6 sc, work FPdc around next 2 FPdc †, sc in next 2 sc, repeat from † to † once, sc in last sc.

Row 9: Repeat Row 5.

Rows 11, 13, 15, and 17: Ch 1, turn; sc in first 4 sc, work FPdc around next 4 FPdc, sc in next 8 sc, work FPdc around next 4 FPdc, sc in last 4 sc.

Repeat Rows 4-17 until piece measures 7" (18 cm) from beginning ch; do **not** finish off.

Work Edging (*see Finishing, page 10*).

19 celtic PLAIT

Ch 26.

Row 1 (Right side)**:** Sc in second ch from hook and in each ch across: 25 sc.

Note: Loop a short piece of yarn around any stitch to mark Row 1 as **right** side and **bottom** edge.

Row 2 AND ALL WRONG SIDE ROWS: Ch 1, turn; sc in each st across.

To work Front Post double crochet (abbreviated FPdc), YO, insert hook from **front** to **back** around post of st indicated (*Fig. 1, page 59*), YO and pull up a loop, (YO and draw through 2 loops on hook) twice. Skip sc **behind** FPdc.

Row 3: Ch 1, turn; sc in first 7 sc, work FPdc around sc one row **below** next sc, (sc in next sc, work FPdc around sc one row **below** next sc) 5 times, sc in last 7 sc.

Row 5: Ch 1, turn; sc in first 8 sc, work FPdc around next FPdc, sc in next sc, work FPdc around next FPdc, skip next FPdc, work FPdc around next FPdc, sc in next sc, working **behind** FPdc just made (*Fig. 3b, page 59*), work FPdc around skipped FPdc, work FPdc around next FPdc, sc in next sc, work FPdc around next FPdc, sc in last 8 sc.

Row 7: Ch 1, turn; sc in first 9 sc, work FPdc around next FPdc, skip next FPdc, work FPdc around next FPdc, working in **front** of FPdc just made (*Fig. 3a, page 59*), work FPdc around skipped FPdc, sc in next sc, skip next FPdc, work FPdc around next FPdc, working in **front** of FPdc just made, work FPdc around skipped FPdc, work FPdc around next FPdc, sc in last 9 sc.

Row 9: Ch 1, turn; sc in first 9 sc, ★ skip next FPdc, work FPdc around next FPdc, working **behind** FPdc just made, work FPdc around skipped FPdc; repeat from ★ 2 times **more**, sc in last 10 sc.

Row 11: Ch 1, turn; sc in first 8 sc, work FPdc around next FPdc, sc in next sc, ★ skip next FPdc, work FPdc around next FPdc, working in **front** of FPdc just made, work FPdc around skipped FPdc, sc in next sc; repeat from ★ once **more**, work FPdc around next FPdc, sc in last 8 sc.

Row 13: Ch 1, turn; sc in first 7 sc, (work FPdc around next FPdc, sc in next sc) twice, skip next FPdc, work FPdc around next FPdc, sc in next sc, working **behind** FPdc just made, work FPdc around skipped FPdc, (sc in next sc, work FPdc around next FPdc) twice, sc in last 7 sc.

Row 15, 17, and 19: Ch 1, turn; sc in first 7 sc, work FPdc around next FPdc, (sc in next sc, work FPdc around next FPdc) 5 times, sc in last 7 sc.

Repeat Rows 4-19 until piece measures 7" (18 cm) from beginning ch; do **not** finish off.

Work Edging (*see Finishing, page 10*).

 **open bobbled CABLES**

Ch 25.

Row 1 (Right side)**:** Hdc in third ch from hook (**2 skipped chs count as first hdc**) and in each ch across: 24 hdc.

Note: Loop a short piece of yarn around any stitch to mark Row 1 as **right** side and **bottom** edge.

Row 2 AND ALL WRONG SIDE ROWS: Ch 2 (counts as first hdc, now and throughout), turn; hdc in next st and in each st across.

To work Front Post double crochet (abbreviated FPdc), YO, insert hook from **front** to **back** around post of st indicated (*Fig. 1, page 59*), YO and pull up a loop even with st on hook, (YO and draw through 2 loops on hook) twice. Skip hdc **behind** FPdc.

Row 3: Ch 2, turn; hdc in next 2 hdc, ★ † skip next 2 hdc, work FPdc around hdc one row **below** next hdc, hdc in next hdc, working in **front** of FPdc just made (*Fig. 3a, page 59*), work FPdc around hdc one row **below** first skipped hdc †, hdc in next 2 hdc; repeat from ★ 2 times **more**, then repeat from † to † once, hdc in last 3 hdc.

Row 5: Ch 2, turn; hdc in next 2 hdc, ★ † work FPdc around next FPdc, hdc in next hdc, work FPdc around next FPdc †, hdc in next 2 hdc; repeat from ★ 2 times **more**, then repeat from † to † once, hdc in last 3 hdc.

To work Popcorn (uses one hdc), 4 hdc in next hdc, drop loop from hook, insert hook in first hdc of 4-hdc group, hook dropped loop and draw through st. Ch 1 to close.

Row 7: Ch 2, turn; hdc in next 2 hdc, ★ † work FPdc around next FPdc, work Popcorn, work FPdc around next FPdc †, hdc in next 2 hdc; repeat from ★ 2 times **more**, then repeat from † to † once, hdc in last 3 hdc.

Row 9: Repeat Row 5.

Row 11: Ch 2, turn; hdc in next 2 hdc, ★ † skip next FPdc, work FPdc around next FPdc, hdc in next hdc, working in **front** of FPdc just made, work FPdc around skipped FPdc †, hdc in next 2 hdc; repeat from ★ 2 times **more**, then repeat from † to † once, hdc in last 3 hdc.

Rows 12-19: Repeat Rows 4-11; do **not** finish off.

Work Edging (*see Finishing, page 10*).

 **chained CABLE**

Ch 25.

Row 1 (Right side)**:** Hdc in third ch from hook (**2 skipped chs count as first hdc**) and in each ch across: 24 hdc.

Note: Loop a short piece of yarn around any stitch to mark Row 1 as **right** side.

Row 2 AND ALL WRONG SIDE ROWS: Ch 2 (counts as first hdc, now and throughout), turn; hdc in next hdc and in each st across.

To work Front Post treble crochet (abbreviated FPtr), YO twice, insert hook from **front** to **back** around post of st indicated (*Fig. 1, page 59*), YO and pull up a loop, (YO and draw through 2 loops on hook) 3 times. Skip hdc **behind** FPtr.

Row 3: Ch 2, turn; hdc in next 4 hdc, † skip next 2 hdc, work FPtr around hdc one row **below** next 2 hdc, working in **front** of FPtr just made (*Fig. 3a, page 59*), work FPtr around each skipped hdc †, hdc in next 6 hdc, repeat from † to † once, hdc in last 5 hdc.

Row 5: Ch 2, turn; hdc in next 3 hdc, ★ work FPtr around next 2 FPtr, hdc in next 2 hdc, work FPtr around next 2 FPtr, hdc in next 4 hdc; repeat from ★ once **more**.

Row 7: Ch 2, turn; hdc in next 2 hdc, † work FPtr around next 2 FPtr, hdc in next 4 hdc, work FPtr around next 2 FPtr †, hdc in next 2 hdc, repeat from † to † once, hdc in last 3 hdc.

Row 9: Ch 2, turn; hdc in next 3 hdc, work FPtr around next 2 FPtr, hdc in next 2 hdc, work FPtr around next FPtr, hdc in next 4 hdc, work FPtr around next 2 FPtr, hdc in next 2 hdc, work FPtr around next 2 FPtr, hdc in last 4 hdc.

Row 11: Ch 2, turn; hdc in next 4 hdc, skip next 2 FPtr, work FPtr around next 2 FPtr, working in **front** of FPtr just made, work FPtr around each skipped FPtr, hdc in next 6 hdc, skip next 2 FPtr, work FPtr around next 2 FPtr, working in **front** of FPtr just made, work FPtr around 2 skipped FPtr, hdc in last 5 hdc.

Rows 12-19: Repeat Rows 4-11; do **not** finish off, mark last row as **bottom** edge.

Work Edging (*see Finishing, page 10*).

chained EIGHT

Ch 25.

Row 1 (Right side)**:** Sc in second ch from hook and in each ch across: 24 sc.

Note: Loop a short piece of yarn around any stitch to mark Row 1 as **right** side and **bottom** edge.

Row 2 AND ALL WRONG SIDE ROWS: Ch 1, turn; sc in each st across.

To work Front Post double crochet (abbreviated FPdc), YO, insert hook from **front** to **back** around post of st indicated (*Fig. 1, page 59*), YO and pull up a loop, (YO and draw through 2 loops on hook) twice. Skip sc **behind** FPdc.

Row 3: Ch 1, turn; sc in first 4 sc, work FPdc around sc one row **below** next 4 sc, sc in next 8 sc, work FPdc around sc one row **below** next 4 sc, sc in last 4 sc.

Row 5: Ch 1, turn; sc in first 4 sc, work FPdc around next 4 FPdc, sc in next 8 sc, work FPdc around next 4 FPdc, sc in last 4 sc.

Row 7: Ch 1, turn; sc in first 3 sc, † work FPdc around next 2 FPdc, sc in next 2 sc, work FPdc around next 2 FPdc †, sc in next 6 sc, repeat from † to † once, sc in last 3 sc.

Row 9: Ch 1, turn; sc in first 2 sc, work FPdc around next 2 FPdc, (sc in next 4 sc, work FPdc around next 2 FPdc) 3 times, sc in last 2 sc.

Row 11: Ch 1, turn; sc in first sc, † work FPdc around next 2 FPdc, sc in next 6 sc, work FPdc around next 2 FPdc †, sc in next 2 sc, repeat from † to † once, sc in last sc.

Row 13: Ch 1, turn; sc in first 2 sc, work FPdc around next 2 FPdc, (sc in next 4 sc, work FPdc around next 2 FPdc) 3 times, sc in last 2 sc.

Row 15: Ch 1, turn; sc in first 3 sc, work FPdc around next 2 FPdc, sc in next 2 sc, work FPdc around next 2 FPdc, sc in next 6 sc, work FPdc around next 2 FPdc, sc in next 2 sc, work FPdc around next 2 FPdc, sc in last 3 sc.

To work Front Post treble crochet (abbreviated FPtr), YO twice, insert hook from **front** to **back** around post of st indicated (*Fig. 1, page 59*), YO and pull up a loop, (YO and draw through 2 loops on hook) 3 times. Skip st **behind** FPtr.

Row 17: Ch 1, turn; sc in first 4 sc, † skip next 2 FPdc, work FPtr around next 2 FPdc, working in **front** of FPtr just made (*Fig. 3a, page 59*), work FPtr around each skipped FPdc †, sc in next 8 sc, repeat from † to † once, sc in last 4 sc.

Row 19: Ch 1, turn; sc in first 3 sc, † work FPtr around next 2 FPtr, sc in next 2 sc, work FPtr around next 2 FPtr †, sc in next 6 sc, repeat from † to † once, sc in last 3 sc.

Rows 20-29: Repeat Rows 8-17; do **not** finish off.

Work Edging (*see Finishing, page 10*).

corded RIB

Ch 24.

Row 1 (Right side)**:** Sc in second ch from hook and in each ch across: 23 sc.

Note: Loop a short piece of yarn around any stitch to mark Row 1 as **right** side and **bottom** edge.

Row 2 AND ALL WRONG SIDE ROWS: Ch 1, turn; sc in each st across.

To work Front Post double crochet (abbreviated FPdc), YO, insert hook from **front** to **back** around post of st indicated (*Fig. 1, page 59*), YO and pull up a loop, (YO and draw through 2 loops on hook) twice. Skip sc **behind** FPdc.

Row 3: Ch 1, turn; sc in first 2 sc, ★ † skip next sc, work FPdc around sc one row **below** next sc, working in **front** of FPdc just made (*Fig. 3a, page 59*), work FPdc around sc one row **below** skipped sc, work FPdc around sc one row **below** next sc †, sc in next sc; repeat from ★ 3 times **more**, then repeat from † to † once, sc in last 2 sc.

Row 5: Ch 1, turn; sc in first 2 sc, ★ † skip next FPdc, work FPdc around next FPdc, working in **front** of FPdc just made, work FPdc around skipped FPdc, work FPdc around next FPdc †, sc in next sc; repeat from ★ 3 times **more**, then repeat from † to † once, sc in last 2 sc.

Repeat Rows 4 and 5 until piece measures 7" (18 cm) from beginning ch; do **not** finish off.

Work Edging (*see Finishing, page 10*).

24 STAGHORN

Ch 25.

Row 1 (Right side)**:** Hdc in third ch from hook (**2 skipped chs count as first hdc**) and in each ch across: 24 hdc.

Note: Loop a short piece of yarn around any stitch to mark Row 1 as **right** side and **bottom** edge.

Row 2 AND ALL WRONG SIDE ROWS: Ch 2 (**counts as first hdc, now and throughout**), turn; hdc in next hdc and in each st across.

To work Front Post double crochet (abbreviated FPdc), YO, insert hook from **front** to **back** around post of st indicated (*Fig. 1, page 59*), YO and pull up a loop even with st on hook, (YO and draw through 2 loops on hook) twice. Skip hdc **behind** FPdc.

Row 3: Ch 2, turn; hdc in next 9 hdc, work FPdc around hdc one row **below** next 4 hdc, hdc in last 10 hdc.

Row 5: Ch 2, turn; hdc in next 8 hdc, work FPdc around next 2 FPdc, hdc in next 2 hdc, work FPdc around next 2 FPdc, hdc in last 9 hdc.

Row 7: Ch 2, turn; hdc in next 6 hdc, work FPdc around next 2 FPdc, hdc in next 2 hdc, work FPdc around hdc one row **below** next 2 hdc, hdc in next 2 hdc, work FPdc around next 2 FPdc, hdc in last 7 hdc.

Row 9: Ch 2, turn; hdc in next 6 hdc, work FPdc around next 2 FPdc, hdc in next hdc, work FPdc around st one row **below** next 4 hdc, hdc in next hdc, work FPdc around next 2 FPdc, hdc in last 7 hdc.

Repeat Rows 4-9 until piece measures 7" (18 cm) from beginning ch; do **not** finish off.

Work Edging (*see Finishing, page 10*).

25 alternating CABLES

Ch 24.

Row 1 (Right side)**:** Hdc in third ch from hook (**2 skipped chs count as first hdc**) and in each ch across: 23 hdc.

Note: Loop a short piece of yarn around any stitch to mark Row 1 as **right** side and **bottom** edge.

Row 2 AND ALL WRONG SIDE ROWS: Ch 2 (**counts as first hdc, now and throughout**), turn; hdc in next st and in each st across.

To work Front Post double crochet (abbreviated FPdc), YO, insert hook from **front** to **back** around post of st indicated (*Fig. 1, page 59*), YO and pull up a loop even with st on hook, (YO and draw through 2 loops on hook) twice. Skip hdc **behind** FPdc.

Row 3: Ch 2, turn; hdc in next hdc, ★ † work FPdc around hdc one row **below** next 2 hdc, hdc in next hdc †, skip next hdc, work FPdc around hdc one row **below** next hdc, working in **front** of last FPdc made (*Fig. 3a, page 59*), work FPdc around hdc one row **below** skipped hdc, hdc in next hdc; repeat from ★ 2 times **more**, then repeat from † to † once.

Row 5: Ch 2, turn; hdc in next hdc, (work FPdc around next 2 FPdc, hdc in next hdc) across.

Row 7: Ch 2, turn; hdc in next hdc, work FPdc around next 2 FPdc, hdc in next hdc, ★ skip next FPdc, work FPdc around next FPdc, working in **front** of FPdc just made, work FPdc around skipped FPdc, hdc in next hdc, work FPdc around next 2 FPdc, hdc in next hdc; repeat from ★ across.

Row 9: Repeat Row 5.

Row 11: Repeat Row 7.

Row 13: Ch 2, turn; hdc in next hdc, ★ † skip next FPdc, work FPdc around next FPdc, working in **front** of FPdc just made, work FPdc around skipped FPdc, hdc in next hdc †, work FPdc around next 2 FPdc, hdc in next hdc; repeat from ★ 2 times **more**, then repeat from † to † once.

Row 15: Repeat Row 5.

Row 17: Repeat Row 13.

Row 19: Repeat Row 5.

Row 21: Repeat Row 13; do **not** finish off.

Work Edging (*see Finishing, page 10*).

bobbled CABLE RIBS

Ch 24.

Row 1 (Right side)**:** Hdc in third ch from hook (**2 skipped chs count as first hdc**) and in each ch across: 23 hdc.

Note: Loop a short piece of yarn around any stitch to mark Row 1 as **right** side and **bottom** edge.

Row 2 AND ALL WRONG SIDE ROWS: Ch 2 (counts as first hdc, now and throughout), turn; hdc in next st and in each st across.

To work Front Post double crochet (abbreviated FPdc), YO, insert hook from **front** to **back** around post of st indicated (**Fig. 1, page 59**), YO and pull up a loop even with st on hook, (YO and draw through 2 loops on hook) twice. Skip hdc **behind** FPdc.

To work Popcorn (uses one hdc), 4 hdc in next hdc, drop loop from hook, insert hook in first hdc of 4-hdc group, hook dropped loop and draw through st. Ch 1 to close.

Row 3: Ch 2, turn; work FPdc around hdc one row **below** next hdc, (work Popcorn, work FPdc around hdc one row **below** next hdc) across to last hdc, hdc in last hdc.

Row 5: Ch 2, turn; work FPdc around next FPdc, (work Popcorn, work FPdc around next FPdc) across to last hdc, hdc in last hdc.

Repeat Rows 4 and 5 until piece measures 7" (18 cm) from beginning ch; do **not** finish off.

Work Edging (*see Finishing, page 10*).

twisted COLUMNS

Ch 24.

Row 1 (Right side)**:** Hdc in third ch from hook (**2 skipped chs count as first hdc**) and in each ch across: 23 hdc.

Note: Loop a short piece of yarn around any stitch to mark Row 1 as **right** side and **bottom** edge.

Row 2 AND ALL WRONG SIDE ROWS: Ch 2 (counts as first hdc, now and throughout), turn; hdc in next st and in each st across.

To work Front Post double crochet (abbreviated FPdc), YO, insert hook from **front** to **back** around post of st indicated (**Fig. 1, page 59**), YO and pull up a loop even with st on hook, (YO and draw through 2 loops on hook) twice. Skip hdc **behind** FPdc.

Row 3: Ch 2, turn; ★ hdc in next hdc, work FPdc around hdc one row **below** next 4 hdc, hdc in next hdc, skip next 2 hdc, work FPdc around hdc one row **below** next 2 hdc, working in **front** of FPdc just made (**Fig. 3a, page 59**), work FPdc around hdc one row **below** each skipped hdc; repeat from ★ once **more**, hdc in last 2 hdc.

Row 5: Ch 2, turn; ★ hdc in next hdc, work FPdc around next 4 FPdc, hdc in next hdc, skip next 2 FPdc, work FPdc around next 2 FPdc, working in **front** of FPdc just made, work FPdc around each skipped FPdc; repeat from ★ once **more**, hdc in last 2 hdc.

Rows 7 and 9: Ch 2, ★ hdc in next hdc, skip next 2 FPdc, work FPdc around next 2 FPdc, working in **front** of FPdc just made, work FPdc around each skipped FPdc, hdc in next hdc, work FPdc around next 4 FPdc; repeat from ★ once **more**, hdc in last 2 hdc.

Rows 11 and 13: Ch 2, turn; ★ hdc in next hdc, work FPdc around next 4 FPdc, hdc in next hdc, skip next 2 FPdc, work FPdc around next 2 FPdc, working in **front** of FPdc just made, work FPdc around each skipped FPdc; repeat from ★ once **more**, hdc in last 2 hdc.

Repeat Rows 6-13 until piece measures 7" (18 cm) from beginning ch; do **not** finish off.

Work Edging (*see Finishing, page 10*).

28 CABLED rope

Ch 24.

Row 1 (Right side)**:** Hdc in third ch from hook
(2 skipped chs count as first hdc) and in each ch across:
23 hdc.

Note: Loop a short piece of yarn around any stitch to
mark Row 1 as **right** side and **bottom** edge.

Row 2 AND ALL WRONG SIDE ROWS: Ch 2 (counts
as first hdc, now and throughout), turn; hdc in next st
and in each st across.

*To work Front Post double crochet (abbreviated
FPdc),* YO, insert hook from **front** to **back** around post
of st indicated (*Fig. 1, page 59*), YO and pull up a loop
even with st on hook, (YO and draw through 2 loops on
hook) twice. Skip hdc **behind** FPdc.

Row 3: Ch 2, turn; hdc in next 2 hdc, ★ work FPdc
around hdc one row **below** next 3 hdc, hdc in next hdc,
work FPdc around hdc one row **below** next 3 hdc, hdc
in next 3 hdc; repeat from ★ once **more**.

Rows 5, 7, and 9: Ch 2, turn; hdc in next 2 hdc,
★ work FPdc around next 3 FPdc, hdc in next hdc,
work FPdc around next 3 FPdc, hdc in next 3 hdc;
repeat from ★ once **more**.

Row 11: Ch 2, turn; hdc in next 2 hdc, ★ skip next
3 FPdc, work FPdc around next 3 FPdc, hdc in next hdc,
working in **front** of FPdc just made (*Fig. 3a, page 59*),
work FPdc around each skipped FPdc, hdc in next
3 hdc; repeat from ★ once **more**.

Row 13: Ch 2, turn; hdc in next 2 hdc, ★ work FPdc
around next 3 hdc, hdc in next hdc, work FPdc around
next 3 hdc, hdc in next 3 hdc; repeat from ★ across.

Row 15: Repeat Row 11.

Row 17: Repeat Row 13.

Row 19: Repeat Row 5; do **not** finish off.

Work Edging (*see Finishing, page 10).*

29 LOZENGE

Ch 24.

Row 1 (Right side)**:** Hdc in third ch from hook
(2 skipped chs count as first hdc) and in each ch across:
23 hdc.

Note: Loop a short piece of yarn around any stitch to
mark Row 1 as **right** side and **bottom** edge.

Row 2 AND ALL WRONG SIDE ROWS: Ch 2 (counts
as first hdc, now and throughout), turn; hdc in next st
and in each st across.

*To work Front Post double crochet (abbreviated
FPdc),* YO, insert hook from **front** to **back** around post
of st indicated (*Fig. 1, page 59*), YO and pull up a loop
even with st on hook, (YO and draw through 2 loops on
hook) twice. Skip hdc **behind** FPdc.

Row 3: Ch 2, turn; ★ hdc in next hdc, skip next 2 hdc,
work FPdc around hdc one row **below** next hdc, hdc
in second skipped hdc, working in **front** of FPdc just
made (*Fig. 3a, page 59*), work FPdc around hdc one
row **below** first skipped hdc; repeat from ★ across to
last 2 hdc, hdc in last 2 hdc.

Rows 5, 7, and 9: Ch 2, turn; ★ † (hdc in next hdc,
work FPdc around next FPdc) twice †, hdc in next hdc,
skip next FPdc, work FPdc around next FPdc, hdc in
next hdc, working in **front** of FPdc just made, work
FPdc around skipped FPdc; repeat from ★ once **more**,
then repeat from † to † once, hdc in last 2 hdc.

Rows 11, 13, and 15: Ch 2, turn; ★ † hdc in next hdc,
skip next FPdc, work FPdc around next FPdc, hdc in
next hdc, working in **front** of FPdc just made, work
FPdc around skipped FPdc †, (hdc in next hdc, work
FPdc around next FPdc) twice; repeat from ★ once
more, then repeat from † to † once, hdc in last 2 hdc.

Rows 17 and 19: Repeat Rows 5 and 7; do **not**
finish off.

Work Edging (*see Finishing, page 10).*

30 triple TWIST

Ch 24.

Row 1 (Right side)**:** Hdc in third ch from hook (**2 skipped chs count as first hdc**) and in each ch across: 23 hdc.

Note: Loop a short piece of yarn around any stitch to mark Row 1 as **right** side and **bottom** edge.

Row 2 AND ALL WRONG SIDE ROWS: Ch 2 (**counts as first hdc, now and throughout**), turn; hdc in next st and in each st across.

To work Front Post double crochet (abbreviated FPdc), YO, insert hook from **front** to **back** around post of st indicated (*Fig. 1, page 59*), YO and pull up a loop even with st on hook, (YO and draw through 2 loops on hook) twice. Skip hdc **behind** FPdc.

Row 3: Ch 2, turn; (hdc in next hdc, work FPdc around hdc one row **below** next 4 hdc) across to last 2 hdc, hdc in last 2 hdc.

Rows 5 and 7: Ch 2, turn; (hdc in next hdc, work FPdc around next 4 FPdc) across to last 2 hdc, hdc in last 2 hdc.

Row 9: Ch 2, turn; ★ hdc in next hdc, [skip next FPdc, work FPdc around next FPdc, working **behind** FPdc just made (*Fig. 3b, page 59*), work FPdc around skipped FPdc] twice; repeat from ★ across to last 2 hdc, hdc in last 2 hdc.

Row 11: Ch 2, turn; ★ hdc in next hdc, work FPdc around next FPdc, skip next FPdc, work FPdc around next FPdc, working **behind** FPdc just made, work FPdc around skipped FPdc, work FPdc around next FPdc; repeat from ★ across to last 2 hdc, hdc in last 2 hdc.

Row 13: Ch 2, turn; ★ hdc in next hdc, (skip next FPdc, work FPdc around next FPdc) twice, working **behind** FPdc just made, work FPdc around each skipped FPdc; repeat from ★ across to last 2 hdc, hdc in last 2 hdc.

Row 15: Ch 2, turn; (hdc in next hdc, work FPdc around next 4 FPdc) across to last 2 hdc, hdc in last 2 hdc.

Repeat Rows 4-15 until piece measures 7" (18 cm) from beginning ch; do **not** finish off.

Work Edging (*see Finishing, page 10*).

31 broken CROSS

Ch 25.

Row 1 (Right side)**:** Sc in second ch from hook and in each ch across: 24 sc.

Note: Loop a short piece of yarn around any stitch to mark Row 1 as **right** side.

Row 2 AND ALL WRONG SIDE ROWS: Ch 1, turn; sc in each st across.

Row 3: Ch 1, turn; sc in each sc across.

To work Front Post treble crochet (abbreviated FPtr), YO twice, insert hook from **front** to **back** around post of st indicated (*Fig. 1, page 59*), YO and pull up a loop, (YO and draw through 2 loops on hook) 3 times. Skip sc **behind** FPtr.

To work Front Post double crochet (abbreviated FPdc), YO, insert hook from **front** to **back** around post of st indicated (*Fig. 1, page 59*), YO and pull up a loop, (YO and draw through 2 loops on hook) twice. Skip sc **behind** FPdc.

Row 5: Ch 1, turn; sc in first 2 sc, † skip next 4 sc, work FPtr around sc 3 rows **below** next 2 sc, sc in third and fourth skipped sc, working in **front** of FPtr just made (*Fig. 3a, page 59*), work FPtr around sc 3 rows **below** first 2 skipped sc †, sc in next 3 sc, work FPdc around sc 3 rows **below** next 2 sc, sc in next 3 sc, repeat from † to † once, sc in last 2 sc.

Row 7: Ch 1, turn; sc in each sc across.

Row 9: Ch 1, turn; sc in first 4 sc, work FPdc around sc 3 rows **below** next 2 sc, sc in next 3 sc, skip next 4 sc, work FPtr around sc 3 rows **below** next 2 sc, sc in third and fourth skipped sc, work FPtr around sc 3 rows **below** first 2 skipped sc, sc in next 3 sc, work FPdc around sc 3 rows **below** next 2 sc, sc in last 4 sc.

Repeat Rows 2-9 until piece measures 7" (18 cm) from beginning ch; do **not** finish off, mark last row as **bottom** edge.

Work Edging (*see Finishing, page 10*).

DIAMOND X

Ch 25.

Row 1 (Right side)**:** Hdc in third ch from hook (**2 skipped chs count as first hdc**) and in each ch across: 24 hdc.

Note: Loop a short piece of yarn around any stitch to mark Row 1 as **right** side and **bottom** edge.

Row 2 AND ALL WRONG SIDE ROWS: Ch 2 (counts as first hdc, now and throughout), turn; hdc in next st and in each st across.

To work Front Post double crochet (abbreviated FPdc), YO, insert hook from **front** to **back** around post of st indicated (*Fig. 1, page 59*), YO and pull up a loop even with st on hook, (YO and draw through 2 loops on hook) twice. Skip hdc **behind** FPdc.

Row 3: Ch 2, turn; hdc in next 9 hdc, skip next 2 hdc, work FPdc around hdc one row **below** next 2 hdc, working in **front** of FPdc just made (*Fig. 3a, page 59*), work FPdc around hdc one row **below** each skipped hdc, hdc in last 10 hdc.

Row 5: Ch 2, turn; hdc in next 8 hdc, work FPdc around next 2 FPdc, hdc in next 2 hdc, work FPdc around next 2 FPdc, hdc in last 9 hdc.

Row 7: Ch 2, turn; hdc in next 7 hdc, work FPdc around next 2 FPdc, hdc in next 4 hdc, work FPdc around next 2 FPdc, hdc in last 8 hdc.

Row 9: Ch 2, turn; hdc in next 6 hdc, work FPdc around next 2 FPdc, hdc in next 6 hdc, work FPdc around next 2 FPdc, hdc in last 7 hdc.

Row 11: Ch 2, turn; hdc in next 5 hdc, work FPdc around next 2 FPdc, hdc in next 8 hdc, work FPdc around next 2 FPdc, hdc in last 6 hdc.

To work Front Post double treble crochet (abbreviated FPdtr), YO 3 times, insert hook from **front** to **back** around post of st indicated (*Fig. 1, page 59*), YO and pull up a loop, (YO and draw through 2 loops on hook) 4 times. Skip hdc **behind** FPdtr.

Row 13: Ch 2, turn; hdc in next 6 hdc, work FPdc around next 2 FPdc, skip next 4 hdc, (work FPdtr around hdc 3 rows **below** next 2 hdc, hdc in third and fourth skipped hdc, work FPdtr around hdc 3 rows **below** first 2 skipped hdc, work FPdc around next 2 FPdc, hdc in last 7 hdc.

Row 15: Ch 2, turn; hdc in next 7 hdc, work FPdc around next 2 FPdc, hdc in next 4 hdc, work FPdc around next 2 FPdc, hdc in last 8 hdc.

Row 17: Ch 2, turn; hdc in next 8 hdc, work FPdc around next 2 FPdc, hdc in next 2 hdc, work FPdc around next 2 FPdc, hdc in last 9 hdc.

Row 19: Ch 2, turn; hdc in next 9 hdc, skip next 2 FPdc, work FPdc around next 2 FPdc, working in **front** of FPdc just made, work FPdc around each skipped FPdc, hdc in last 10 hdc; do **not** finish off.

Work Edging (*see Finishing, page 10*).

copycat CABLE

Ch 24.

Row 1 (Right side)**:** Sc in second ch from hook and in each ch across: 23 sc.

Note: Loop a short piece of yarn around any stitch to mark Row 1 as **right** side and **bottom** edge.

Row 2 AND ALL WRONG SIDE ROWS: Ch 1, turn; sc in each st across.

To work Front Post double crochet (abbreviated FPdc), YO, insert hook from **front** to **back** around post of st indicated (*Fig. 1, page 59*), YO and pull up a loop, (YO and draw through 2 loops on hook) twice. Skip sc **behind** FPdc.

Row 3: Ch 1, turn; sc in first 2 sc, work FPdc around sc one row **below** next sc, ★ sc in next 3 sc, skip next sc, work FPdc around sc one row **below** next sc, working in **front** of FPdc just made (*Fig. 3a, page 59*), work FPdc around sc one row **below** skipped sc, sc in next 3 sc, work FPdc around sc one row **below** next sc; repeat from ★ once **more**, sc in last 2 sc.

Row 5: Ch 1, turn; sc in first 2 sc, (work FPdc around next FPdc, sc in next 2 sc) across.

Row 7: Ch 1, turn; sc in first 2 sc, work FPdc around next FPdc, ★ sc in next sc, work FPdc around next FPdc, sc in next 4 sc, work FPdc around next FPdc, sc in next sc, work FPdc around next FPdc; repeat from ★ once **more**, sc in last 2 sc.

Row 9: Ch 1, turn; sc in first 2 sc, (work FPdc around next FPdc, sc in next 2 sc) across.

Row 11: Ch 1, turn; sc in first 2 sc, work FPdc around next FPdc, ★ sc in next 3 sc, work FPdc around next 2 FPdc, sc in next 3 sc, work FPdc around next FPdc; repeat from ★ once **more**, sc in last 2 sc.

Row 13: Ch 1, turn; sc in first 2 sc, work FPdc around next FPdc, ★ sc in next 3 sc, skip next FPdc, work FPdc around next FPdc, working in **front** of FPdc just made, work FPdc around skipped FPdc, sc in next 3 sc, work FPdc around next FPdc; repeat from ★ once **more**, sc in last 2 sc.

Row 15: Ch 1, turn; sc in first 2 sc, (work FPdc around next FPdc, sc in next 2 sc) across.

Row 17: Ch 1, turn; sc in first 2 sc, work FPdc around next FPdc, ★ sc in next 3 sc, work FPdc around next 2 FPdc, sc in next 3 sc, work FPdc around next FPdc; repeat from ★ once **more**, sc in last 2 sc.

Row 19: Ch 1, turn; sc in first 2 sc, work FPdc around next FPdc, sc in next 2 sc, ★ skip next FPdc, work FPdc around next FPdc, sc in next 2 sc, working in **front** of FPdc just made, work FPdc around skipped FPdc, sc in next 2 sc, work FPdc around next FPdc, sc in next 2 sc; repeat from ★ once **more**.

Rows 20-27: Repeat Rows 6-13; do **not** finish off.

Work Edging (see *Finishing, page 10*).

34 twisted DIAMONDS

Ch 25.

Row 1 (Right side): Hdc in third ch from hook (**2 skipped chs count as first hdc**) and in each ch across: 24 hdc.

Note: Loop a short piece of yarn around any stitch to mark Row 1 as **right** side and **bottom** edge.

Row 2 AND ALL WRONG SIDE ROWS: Ch 2 (counts as first hdc, now and throughout), turn; hdc in next st and in each st across.

To work Front Post double crochet (abbreviated FPdc), YO, insert hook from **front** to **back** around post of st indicated (*Fig. 1, page 59*), YO and pull up a loop even with st on hook, (YO and draw through 2 loops on hook) twice. Skip hdc **behind** FPdc.

Row 3: Ch 2, turn; ★ hdc in next 4 hdc, skip next hdc, work FPdc around hdc one row **below** next hdc, working in **front** of FPdc just made (*Fig. 3a, page 59*), work FPdc around hdc one row **below** skipped hdc; repeat from ★ 2 times **more**, hdc in last 5 hdc.

Row 5: Ch 2, turn; (hdc in next 4 hdc, work FPdc around next 2 FPdc) 3 times, hdc in last 5 hdc.

Row 7: Ch 2, turn; ★ hdc in next 4 hdc, skip next FPdc, work FPdc around next FPdc, working in **front** of FPdc just made, work FPdc around skipped FPdc; repeat from ★ 2 times **more**, hdc in last 5 hdc.

Row 9: Ch 2, turn; hdc in next 3 hdc, work FPdc around next FPdc, (hdc in next 2 hdc, work FPdc around next FPdc) across to last 4 hdc, hdc in last 4 hdc.

Row 11: Ch 2, turn; hdc in next 2 hdc, work FPdc around next FPdc, hdc in next 4 hdc, (work FPdc around next 2 FPdc, hdc in next 4 hdc) twice, work FPdc around next FPdc, hdc in last 3 hdc.

Row 13: Ch 2, turn; hdc in next 3 hdc, work FPdc around next FPdc, hdc in next 2 hdc, ★ skip next FPdc, work FPdc around next FPdc, hdc in next 2 hdc, working in **front** of FPdc just made, work FPdc around skipped FPdc, hdc in next 2 hdc; repeat from ★ once **more**, work FPdc around next FPdc, hdc in last 4 hdc.

Row 15: Ch 2, turn; (hdc in next 4 hdc, work FPdc around next 2 FPdc) 3 times, hdc in last 5 hdc.

Row 17: Repeat Row 7.

Row 19: Repeat Row 5; do **not** finish off.

Work Edging (see *Finishing, page 10*).

35 chained DIAMONDS

Ch 25.

Row 1 (Right side)**:** Sc in second ch from hook and in each ch across: 24 sc.

Note: Loop a short piece of yarn around any stitch to mark Row 1 as **right** side and **bottom** edge.

Row 2 AND ALL WRONG SIDE ROWS: Ch 1, turn; sc in each st across.

To work Front Post double crochet (abbreviated FPdc), YO, insert hook from **front** to **back** around post of st indicated (*Fig. 1, page 59*), YO and pull up a loop, (YO and draw through 2 loops on hook) twice. Skip sc **behind** FPdc.

Row 3: Ch 1, turn; sc in first 11 sc, skip next sc, work FPdc around sc one row **below** next sc, working in **front** of FPdc just made (*Fig. 3a, page 59*), work FPdc around sc one row **below** skipped sc, sc in last 11 sc.

Row 5: Ch 1, turn; sc in first 10 sc, work FPdc around next FPdc, sc in next 2 sc, work FPdc around next FPdc, sc in last 10 sc.

Row 7: Ch 1, turn; sc in first 9 sc, work FPdc around next FPdc, sc in next 4 sc, work FPdc around next FPdc, sc in last 9 sc.

Row 9: Ch 1, turn; sc in first 8 sc, work FPdc around next FPdc, sc in next 2 sc, skip next sc, work FPdc around sc one row **below** next sc, working in **front** of FPdc just made, work FPdc around sc one row **below** skipped sc, sc in next 2 sc, work FPdc around next FPdc, sc in last 8 sc.

Row 11: Ch 1, turn; sc in first 7 sc, work FPdc around next FPdc, (sc in next 2 sc, work FPdc around next FPdc) 3 times, sc in last 7 sc.

Row 13: Ch 1, turn; sc in first 7 sc, work FPdc around next FPdc, sc in next sc, work FPdc around next FPdc, sc in next 4 sc, work FPdc around next FPdc, sc in next sc, work FPdc around next FPdc, sc in last 7 sc.

Row 15: Ch 1, turn; sc in first 8 sc, skip next FPdc, work FPdc around next FPdc, working in **front** of FPdc just made, work FPdc around skipped FPdc, sc in next 4 sc, skip next FPdc, work FPdc around next FPdc, working in **front** of FPdc just made, work FPdc around skipped FPdc, sc in last 8 sc.

30

Row 17: Ch 1, turn; sc in first 7 sc, † work FPdc around next FPdc, sc in next 2 sc, work FPdc around next FPdc †, sc in next 2 sc, repeat from † to † once, sc in last 7 sc.

Row 19: Ch 1, turn; sc in first 7 sc, work FPdc around next FPdc, sc in next 3 sc, skip next FPdc, work FPdc around next FPdc, working in **front** of FPdc just made, work FPdc around skipped FPdc, sc in next 3 sc, work FPdc around next FPdc, sc in last 7 sc.

Row 21: Ch 1, turn; sc in first 8 sc, work FPdc around next FPdc, sc in next 6 sc, work FPdc around next FPdc, sc in last 8 sc.

Row 23: Ch 1, turn; sc in first 9 sc, work FPdc around next FPdc, sc in next 4 sc, work FPdc around next FPdc, sc in last 9 sc.

Row 25: Ch 1, turn; sc in first 10 sc, work FPdc around next FPdc, sc in next 2 sc, work FPdc around next FPdc, sc in last 10 sc.

Row 27: Ch 1, turn; sc in first 11 sc, skip next FPdc, work FPdc around next FPdc, working in **front** of FPdc just made, work FPdc around skipped FPdc, sc in last 11 sc; do **not** finish off.

Work Edging (*see Finishing, page 10*).

36 lattice RIB

Ch 25.

Row 1 (Right side)**:** Sc in second ch from hook and in each ch across: 24 sc.

Note: Loop a short piece of yarn around any stitch to mark Row 1 as **right** side and **bottom** edge.

Row 2 AND ALL WRONG SIDE ROWS: Ch 1, turn; sc in each st across.

To work Front Post double crochet (abbreviated FPdc), YO, insert hook from **front** to **back** around post of st indicated (*Fig. 1, page 59*), YO and pull up a loop, (YO and draw through 2 loops on hook) twice. Skip sc **behind** FPdc.

Row 3: Ch 1, turn; sc in first sc, work FPdc around sc one row **below** next 2 sc, (sc in next 2 sc, work FPdc around sc one row **below** next 2 sc) across to last sc, sc in last sc.

Rows 5 and 7: Ch 1, turn; sc in first sc, work FPdc around next 2 FPdc, (sc in next 2 sc, work FPdc around next 2 FPdc) across to last sc, sc in last sc.

Row 9: Ch 1, turn; sc in first sc, work FPdc around next FPdc, sc in next sc, ★ † skip next FPdc, work FPdc around next FPdc, working in **front** of FPdc just made (*Fig. 3a, page 59*), work FPdc around skipped FPdc †, sc in next 2 sc; repeat from ★ 3 times **more**, then repeat from † to † once, sc in next sc, work FPdc around next FPdc, sc in last sc.

Row 11: Ch 1, turn; sc in first sc, work FPdc around next 2 FPdc, (sc in next 2 sc, work FPdc around next 2 FPdc) 5 times, sc in last sc.

Row 13: Ch 1, turn; sc in first sc, work FPdc around next 2 FPdc, sc in next 2 sc, ★ skip next FPdc, work FPdc around next FPdc, working in **front** of FPdc just made, work FPdc around skipped FPdc, sc in next 2 sc; repeat from ★ 3 times **more**, work FPdc around next 2 FPdc, sc in last sc.

Rows 15, 17, and 19: Ch 1, turn; sc in first sc, work FPdc around next 2 FPdc, (sc in next 2 sc, work FPdc around next 2 FPdc) across to last sc, sc in last sc.

Repeat Rows 8-19 until piece measures 7" (18 cm) from beginning ch; do **not** finish off.

Work Edging (*see Finishing, page 10*).

37 berry TREE

Ch 25.

Row 1 (Right side)**:** Sc in second ch from hook and in each ch across: 24 sc.

Note: Loop a short piece of yarn around any stitch to mark Row 1 as **right** side and **bottom** edge.

Row 2: Ch 1, turn; sc in each st across.

To work Front Post double crochet (abbreviated FPdc), YO, insert hook from **front** to **back** around post of st indicated (*Fig. 1, page 59*), YO and pull up a loop, (YO and draw through 2 loops on hook) twice. Skip sc **behind** FPdc.

Row 3: Ch 1, turn; sc in first 3 sc, work FPdc around sc one row **below** next sc, sc in next 5 sc, † skip next sc, work FPdc around sc one row **below** next sc, working **behind** FPdc just made (*Fig. 3b, page 59*), work FPdc around sc one row **below** skipped sc †, work FPdc around sc one row **below** next 2 sc, repeat from † to † once, sc in next 5 sc, work FPdc around sc one row **below** next sc, sc in last 3 sc.

Row 4: Ch 1, turn; sc in each st across.

Row 5: Ch 1, turn; sc in first 3 sc, work FPdc around next FPdc, sc in next 4 sc, work FPdc around next 2 FPdc, (sc in next sc, work FPdc around next 2 FPdc) twice, sc in next 4 sc, work FPdc around next FPdc, sc in last 3 sc.

Row 6: Ch 1, turn; sc in each st across.

Row 7: Ch 1, turn; sc in first 3 sc, work FPdc around next FPdc, sc in next 3 sc, work FPdc around next 2 FPdc, (sc in next 2 sc, work FPdc around next 2 FPdc) twice, sc in next 3 sc, work FPdc around next FPdc, sc in last 3 sc.

To work Popcorn (uses one sc), 5 sc in next sc, drop loop from hook, insert hook in first sc of 5-sc group, hook dropped loop and draw through st. Ch 1 to close. Push Popcorn to **right** side of work.

Row 8: Ch 1, turn; sc in first 7 sc, work Popcorn, sc in next 7 sc, work Popcorn, sc in last 8 sc.

Row 9: Ch 1, turn; sc in first 3 sc, (work FPdc around next FPdc, sc in next 3 sts) twice, work FPdc around next 2 FPdc, sc in next 3 sts, (work FPdc around next FPdc, sc in next 3 sc) twice.

Row 10: Ch 1, turn; sc in first 6 sc, work Popcorn, sc in next 9 sc, work Popcorn, sc in last 7 sc.

Row 11: Ch 1, turn; sc in first 3 sc, work FPdc around next FPdc, sc in next 5 sts, † skip next sc, work FPdc around sc one row **below** next sc, working **behind** FPdc just made, work FPdc around sc one row **below** skipped sc †, work FPdc around next 2 FPdc, repeat from † to † once, sc in next 5 sts, work FPdc around next FPdc, sc in last 3 sc.

Repeat Rows 4-11 until piece measures 7" (18 cm) from beginning ch; do **not** finish off.

Work Edging (*see Finishing, page 10*).

round the COLUMNS

Ch 24.

Row 1 (Right side)**:** Sc in second ch from hook and in each ch across: 23 sc.

Note: Loop a short piece of yarn around any stitch to mark Row 1 as **right** side and **bottom** edge.

Row 2 AND ALL WRONG SIDE ROWS: Ch 1, turn; sc in each st across.

To work Front Post double crochet (abbreviated FPdc), YO, insert hook from **front** to **back** around post of st indicated (*Fig. 1, page 59*), YO and pull up a loop, (YO and draw through 2 loops on hook) twice. Skip sc **behind** FPdc.

Row 3: Ch 1, turn; sc in first 4 sc, † work FPdc around sc one row **below** next sc, sc in next 5 sc, work FPdc around sc one row **below** next sc †, sc in next sc, repeat from † to † once, sc in last 4 sc.

To work Front Post triple treble crochet (abbreviated FPtr tr), YO 4 times, insert hook from **front** to **back** around post of st indicated (*Fig. 1, page 59*), YO and pull up a loop, (YO and draw through 2 loops on hook) 5 times. Skip sc **behind** FPtr tr.

Row 5: Ch 1, turn; sc in first 4 sc, work FPdc around next FPdc, sc in next 2 sc, skip next FPdc, work FPtr tr around same st on Row 1 as next FPdc, sc in next 2 sc, work FPdc around next FPdc, sc in next sc, work FPdc around next FPdc, sc in next 2 sc, working in **front** of last FPtr tr made (*Fig. 3a, page 59*), work FPtr tr around same st on Row 1 as skipped FPdc, sc in next 2 sc, work FPdc around next FPdc, sc in last 4 sc.

Row 7: Ch 1, turn; sc in first 4 sc, † work FPdc around next FPdc, sc in next 2 sc, work FPdc around next FPtr tr, sc in next 2 sc, work FPdc around next FPdc †, sc in next sc, repeat from † to † once, sc in last 4 sc.

Rows 9 and 11: Ch 1, turn; sc in first 4 sc, † work FPdc around next FPdc, (sc in next 2 sc, work FPdc around next FPdc) twice †, sc in next sc, repeat from † to † once, sc in last 4 sc.

Row 13: Ch 1, turn; sc in first 4 sc, work FPdc around next FPdc, sc in next 5 sc, skip next 3 FPdc, work FPtr tr around next FPdc, sc in next sc, working in **front** of last FPtr tr made, work FPtr tr around first skipped FPdc, sc in next 5 sc, work FPdc around next FPdc, sc in last 4 sc.

Row 15: Ch 1, turn; sc in first 4 sc, work FPdc around next FPdc, sc in next 5 sc, working in **front** of FPtr tr, work FPdc around next skipped FPdc 3 rows **below** next sc, sc in next sc, work FPdc around next skipped FPdc 3 rows **below** next sc, sc in next 5 sc, work FPdc around next FPdc, sc in last 4 sc.

Row 17: Ch 1, turn; sc in first 4 sc, work FPdc around next FPdc, sc in next 2 sc, skip next FPdc, work FPtr tr around next FPdc, sc in next 2 sc, working **behind** last FPtr tr made (*Fig. 3b, page 59*), work FPdc around skipped FPdc, sc in next sc, work FPdc around **same** FPdc as FPtr tr worked, sc in next 2 sc, working in **front** of last FPtr tr made, work FPtr tr around **same** FPdc behind first FPtr tr made, sc in next 2 sc, work FPdc around next FPdc, sc in last 4 sc.

Repeat Rows 6-17 until piece measures 7" (18 cm) from beginning ch; do **not** finish off.

Work Edging (*see Finishing, page 10*).

wheat SHEAF

Ch 24.

Row 1 (Right side)**:** Sc in second ch from hook and in each ch across: 23 sc.

Note: Loop a short piece of yarn around any stitch to mark Row 1 as **right** side and **bottom** edge.

Row 2 AND ALL WRONG SIDE ROWS: Ch 1, turn; sc in each st across.

To work Front Post double crochet (abbreviated FPdc), YO, insert hook from **front** to **back** around post of st indicated (*Fig. 1, page 59*), YO and pull up a loop, (YO and draw through 2 loops on hook) twice. Skip sc **behind** FPdc.

Row 3: Ch 1, turn; sc in first sc, work FPdc around sc one row **below** next sc, (sc in next sc, work FPdc around sc one row **below** next sc) 4 times, sc in next 3 sc, (work FPdc around sc one row **below** next sc, sc in next sc) across.

To work Front Post treble crochet (abbreviated FPtr), YO twice, insert hook from **front** to **back** around post of st indicated *(Fig. 1, page 59)*, YO and pull up a loop, (YO and draw through 2 loops on hook) 3 times. Skip sc **behind** FPtr.

Row 5: Ch 1, turn; sc in first 3 sc, † skip next 2 FPdc, work FPtr around next 3 FPdc, working **behind** FPtr just made *(Fig. 3b, page 59)*, work FPtr around each skipped FPdc †, sc in next 7 sc, repeat from † to † once, sc in last 3 sc.

Row 7: Ch 1, turn; sc in first sc, † work FPdc around next FPtr, (sc in next sc, work FPdc around next FPtr) 4 times †, sc in next 3 sc, repeat from † to † once, sc in last sc.

Row 9: Ch 1, turn; sc in each sc across.

Repeat Rows 2-9 until piece measures 7" (18 cm) from beginning ch; do **not** finish off.

Work Edging *(see Finishing, page 10)*.

40 CABLED bell

Ch 25.

Row 1 (Right side)**:** Hdc in third ch from hook **(2 skipped chs count as first hdc)** and in each ch across: 24 hdc.

Note: Loop a short piece of yarn around any stitch to mark Row 1 as **right** side and **bottom** edge.

Row 2 AND ALL WRONG SIDE ROWS: Ch 2 (counts as first hdc, now and throughout), turn; hdc in next st and in each st across.

Row 3: Ch 2, turn; hdc in next hdc and in each hdc across.

To work Front Post double crochet (abbreviated FPdc), YO, insert hook from **front** to **back** around post of st indicated *(Fig. 1, page 59)*, YO and pull up a loop even with st on hook, (YO and draw through 2 loops on hook) twice. Skip hdc **behind** FPdc.

Row 5: Ch 2, turn; hdc in next 6 hdc, work FPdc around hdc one row **below** next 2 hdc, (hdc in next 2 hdc, work FPdc around hdc one row **below** next 2 hdc) twice, hdc in last 7 hdc.

Rows 7, 9, and 11: Ch 2, turn; hdc in next 6 hdc, work FPdc around next 2 FPdc, (hdc in next 2 hdc, work FPdc around next 2 FPdc) twice, hdc in last 7 hdc.

To work Front Post treble crochet (abbreviated FPtr), YO twice, insert hook from **front** to **back** around post of st indicated *(Fig. 1, page 59)*, YO and pull up a loop, (YO and draw through 2 loops on hook) 3 times. Skip st **behind** FPtr.

Row 13: Ch 2, turn; hdc in next 8 hdc, skip next 3 FPdc, work FPtr around next 3 FPdc, working in **front** of FPtr just made *(Fig. 3a, page 59)*, work FPtr around each skipped FPdc, hdc in last 9 hdc.

Row 15: Ch 2, turn; hdc in next 8 hdc, work FPdc around next 6 FPtr, hdc in last 9 hdc.

Row 17: Ch 2, turn; hdc in next 8 hdc, skip next 3 FPdc, work FPtr around next 3 FPdc, working in **front** of FPtr just made, work FPtr around each skipped FPdc, hdc in last 9 hdc.

Row 19: Ch 2, turn; hdc in next hdc and in each hdc across; do **not** finish off.

Work Edging *(see Finishing, page 10)*.

bobbled ROUNDS

Ch 24.

Row 1 (Right side)**:** Sc in second ch from hook and in each ch across: 23 sc.

Note: Loop a short piece of yarn around any stitch to mark Row 1 as **right** side and **bottom** edge.

Row 2: Ch 1, turn; sc in each st across.

To work Front Post double crochet (abbreviated FPdc), YO, insert hook from **front** to **back** around post of st indicated *(Fig. 1, page 59)*, YO and pull up a loop, (YO and draw through 2 loops on hook) twice. Skip sc **behind** FPdc unless otherwise instructed.

Row 3: Ch 1, turn; sc in first 4 sc, † skip next sc, work FPdc around sc one row **below** next 2 sc, skip next sc **behind** FPdc, sc in next 3 sc, work FPdc around same st as last FPdc made, work FPdc around sc one row **below** next sc, skip next sc **behind** FPdc †, sc in next 5 sc; repeat from † to † once, sc in last 4 sc: 27 sts.

Row 4: Ch 1, turn; sc in first 4 sc, (skip next FPdc, sc in next 5 sts) across to last 5 sts, skip next FPdc, sc in last 4 sc: 23 sc.

Row 5: Ch 1, turn; sc in first 3 sc, (work FPdc around next 2 FPdc, sc in next 3 sc) across.

Row 6 AND ALL WRONG SIDE ROWS THROUGH ROW 12: Ch 1, turn; sc in each st across.

To work Popcorn (uses one sc), 5 dc in next sc, drop loop from hook, insert hook in first dc of 5-dc group, hook dropped loop and draw through st. Ch 1 to close.

Row 7: Ch 1, turn; sc in first 2 sc, † work FPdc around next 2 FPdc, sc in next 2 sc, work Popcorn, sc in next 2 sc, work FPdc around next 2 FPdc †, sc in next sc, repeat from † to † once, sc in last 2 sc.

Row 9: Ch 1, turn; sc in first 3 sc, (work FPdc around next 2 FPdc, sc in next 3 sc) across.

To work Front Post treble crochet (abbreviated FPtr), YO twice, insert hook from **front** to **back** around post of st indicated *(Fig. 1, page 59)*, YO and pull up a loop, (YO and draw through 2 loops on hook) 3 times. Skip sc **behind** FPtr.

Row 11: Ch 1, turn; sc in first 4 sc, † skip next 2 FPdc, work FPtr around next 2 FPdc, sc in next sc, working in **front** of FPtr just made *(Fig. 3a, page 59)*, work FPtr around each skipped FPdc †, sc in next 5 sc, repeat from † to † once, sc in last 4 sc.

Row 13: Ch 1, turn; sc in first 4 sc, † work FPdc around next 2 FPtr, skip next sc **behind** FPdc, sc in next 3 sc, work FPdc around **same** FPtr as last FPdc made and around next FPtr †, sc in next 5 sc, repeat from † to † once, sc in last 4 sc: 27 sts.

Row 14: Ch 1, turn; sc in first 4 sc, (skip next FPdc, sc in next 5 sts) across to last 5 sts, skip next FPdc, sc in last 4 sc: 23 sc.

Row 15: Ch 1, turn; sc in first 3 sc, (work FPdc around next 2 FPdc, sc in next 3 sc) across.

Repeat Rows 6-15 until piece measures 7" (18 cm) from beginning ch; do **not** finish off.

Work Edging *(see Finishing, page 10)*.

CABLED bouquet

Ch 24.

Row 1 (Right side)**:** Hdc in third ch from hook (2 skipped chs count as first hdc) and in each ch across: 23 hdc.

Note: Loop a short piece of yarn around any stitch to mark Row 1 as **right** side and **bottom** edge.

Row 2 AND ALL WRONG SIDE ROWS: Ch 2 (counts as first hdc, now and throughout), turn; hdc in next st and in each st across.

To work Front Post double crochet (abbreviated FPdc), YO, insert hook from **front** to **back** around post of st indicated *(Fig. 1, page 59)*, YO and pull up a loop even with st on hook, (YO and draw through 2 loops on hook) twice. Skip hdc **behind** FPdc.

Row 3: Ch 2, turn; hdc in next 10 hdc, work FPdc around hdc one row **below** next hdc, hdc in last 11 hdc.

Row 5: Ch 2, turn; hdc in next 9 hdc, work FPdc around st one row **below** next 3 hdc, hdc in last 10 hdc.

Row 7: Ch 2, turn; hdc in next 8 hdc, work FPdc around st one row **below** next 5 hdc, hdc in last 9 hdc.

Row 9: Ch 2, turn; hdc in next 8 hdc, work FPdc around next 5 FPdc, hdc in last 9 hdc.

To work Front Post treble crochet (abbreviated FPtr), YO twice, insert hook from **front** to **back** around post of st indicated *(Fig. 1, page 59),* YO and pull up a loop, (YO and draw through 2 loops on hook) 3 times. Skip st **behind** FPtr.

Row 11: Ch 2, turn; hdc in next 8 hdc, skip next 3 FPdc, work FPtr around next 2 FPdc, working in **front** of FPtr just made *(Fig. 3a, page 59),* work FPtr around each skipped FPdc, hdc in last 9 hdc.

Row 13: Ch 2, turn; hdc in next 7 hdc, work FPdc around next FPtr, hdc in next hdc, work FPdc around next 3 FPtr, hdc in next hdc, work FPdc around next FPtr, hdc in last 8 hdc.

To work Popcorn (uses one FPdc), work 5 FPdc around next FPdc, drop loop from hook, insert hook in first FPdc of 5-FPdc group, hook dropped loop and draw through st. Ch 1 to close. Skip hdc **behind** Popcorn.

Row 15: Ch 2, turn; hdc in next 6 hdc, work Popcorn, hdc in next hdc, (work FPdc around next FPdc, hdc in next hdc) 3 times, work Popcorn, hdc in last 7 hdc.

Row 17: Ch 2, turn; hdc in next 8 hdc, work Popcorn, hdc in next hdc, work FPdc around next FPdc, hdc in next hdc, work Popcorn, hdc in last 9 hdc.

Row 19: Ch 2, turn; hdc in next 10 hdc, work Popcorn, hdc in last 11 hdc; do **not** finish off.

Work Edging *(see Finishing, page 10).*

Optional: Wrap a 14" (35.5 cm) length of yarn around FPtr on Row 11 and tie in a bow.

43 CABLED
V'S

Ch 25.

Row 1 (Right side)**:** Hdc in third ch from hook (2 skipped chs count as first hdc) and in each ch across: 24 hdc.

Note: Loop a short piece of yarn around any stitch to mark Row 1 as **right** side and **bottom** edge.

Row 2 AND ALL WRONG SIDE ROWS: Ch 2 (counts as first hdc, now and throughout), turn; hdc in next st and in each st across.

To work Front Post treble crochet (abbreviated FPtr), YO twice, insert hook from **front** to **back** around post of st indicated *(Fig. 1, page 59),* YO and pull up a loop, (YO and draw through 2 loops on hook) 3 times. Skip hdc **behind** FPtr.

Row 3: Ch 2, turn; hdc in next 3 hdc, † skip next 2 hdc, work FPtr around hdc one row **below** next 2 hdc, working in **front** of FPtr just made *(Fig. 3a, page 59),* work FPtr around hdc one row **below** each skipped hdc †, hdc in next 8 hdc, repeat from † to † once, hdc in last 4 hdc.

Row 5: Ch 2, turn; hdc in next 2 hdc, † work FPtr around next 2 FPtr, hdc in next 2 hdc, work FPtr around next 2 FPtr †, hdc in next 6 hdc, repeat from † to † once, hdc in last 3 hdc.

Row 7: Ch 2, turn; hdc in next hdc, work FPtr around next 2 FPtr, (hdc in next 4 hdc, work FPtr around next 2 FPtr) across to last 2 hdc, hdc in last 2 hdc.

Row 9: Ch 2, turn; † work FPtr around next 2 FPtr, hdc in next hdc, skip next 2 hdc, work FPtr around hdc one row **below** next 2 hdc, working in **front** of FPtr just made, work FPtr around hdc one row **below** each skipped hdc, hdc in next hdc, work FPtr around next 2 FPtr †, hdc in next 2 hdc, repeat from † to † once, hdc in last hdc.

Repeat Rows 4-9 until piece measures 7" (18 cm) from beginning ch; do **not** finish off.

Work Edging *(see Finishing, page 10).*

44 BLACKBERRIES

Ch 25.

Row 1 (Right side)**:** Sc in second ch from hook and in each ch across: 24 sc.

Note: Loop a short piece of yarn around any stitch to mark Row 1 as **right** side.

Row 2 AND ALL WRONG SIDE ROWS: Ch 1, turn; sc in each st across.

To work Popcorn (uses one sc), 5 sc in next sc, drop loop from hook, insert hook in first sc of 5-sc group, hook dropped loop and draw through st. Ch 1 to close.

Row 3: Ch 1, turn; sc in first 6 sc, work Popcorn, sc in next 10 sc, work Popcorn, sc in last 6 sc.

To work Front Post double crochet (abbreviated FPdc), YO, insert hook from **front** to **back** around post of st indicated *(Fig. 1, page 59)*, YO and pull up a loop, (YO and draw through 2 loops on hook) twice. Skip sc **behind** FPdc.

Row 5: Ch 1, turn; sc in first 4 sc, † work Popcorn, sc in next sc, work FPdc around top of next Popcorn, sc in next sc, work Popcorn †, sc in next 6 sc, repeat from † to † once, sc in last 4 sc.

Row 7: Ch 1, turn; sc in first 2 sc, ★ work Popcorn, sc in next 3 sc, work FPdc around next FPdc, sc in next 3 sc, work Popcorn, sc in next 2 sc; repeat from ★ once **more**.

To work Front Post treble crochet decrease (abbreviated FPtr decrease), ★ YO twice, insert hook from **front** to **back** around top of **next** Popcorn, YO and pull up a loop, (YO and draw through 2 loops on hook) twice; repeat from ★ once **more**, YO and draw through all 3 loops on hook. Skip sc **behind** FPtr decrease.

Row 9: Ch 1, turn; sc in first 6 sc, ★ work FPtr decrease, work FPdc around next FPdc, skip next Popcorn, work FPtr decrease, sc in next 6 sc; repeat from ★ once **more**.

Row 11: Ch 1, turn; sc in first 7 sc, † YO, skip first FPtr decrease, insert hook from **front** to **back** around first post of second FPtr decrease, YO and pull up a loop, YO and draw through 2 loops on hook, YO, insert hook from **front** to **back** around second post of same FPtr decrease, YO and pull up a loop, YO and draw through 2 loops on hook, YO and draw through all 3 loops on hook, YO, working in **front** of last st made *(Fig. 3a, page 59)*, insert hook from **front** to **back** around first post of first FPtr decrease, YO and pull up a loop, YO and draw through 2 loops on hook, YO, insert hook from **front** to **back** around second post of same FPtr decrease, YO and pull up a loop, YO and draw through 2 loops on hook, YO and draw through all 3 loops on hook *(Cluster made)*, skip sc **behind** Cluster †, sc in next 8 sc, repeat from † to † once, sc in last 7 sc.

Row 13: Ch 1, turn; sc in first 7 sc, † YO, insert hook from **front** to **back** around third post of Cluster, YO and pull up a loop, YO and draw through 2 loops on hook, YO, insert hook from **front** to **back** around fourth post of same st, YO and pull up a loop, YO and draw through 2 loops on hook, YO and draw through all 3 loops on hook, YO, insert hook from **front** to **back** around first post of same st, YO and pull up a loop, YO and draw through 2 loops on hook, YO, insert hook from **front** to **back** around second post of same st, YO and pull up a loop, YO and draw through 2 loops on hook, YO and draw through all 3 loops on hook, skip sc **behind** st just made †, sc in next 8 sc, repeat from † to † once, sc in last 7 sc.

Row 15: Ch 1, turn; sc in each sc across.

Repeat Rows 2-15 until piece measures 7" (18 cm) from beginning ch; do **not** finish off, mark last row as **bottom** edge.

Work Edging *(see Finishing, page 10)*.

45 roaming CABLE

Ch 25.

Row 1 (Right side)**:** Hdc in third ch from hook **(2 skipped chs count as first hdc)** and in each ch across: 24 hdc.

Note: Loop a short piece of yarn around any stitch to mark Row 1 as **right** side.

Row 2 AND ALL WRONG SIDE ROWS: Ch 2 (counts as first hdc, now and throughout), turn; hdc in next st and in each st across.

To work Front Post double crochet (abbreviated FPdc), YO, insert hook from **front** to **back** around post of st indicated (*Fig. 1, page 59*), YO and pull up a loop even with st on hook, (YO and draw through 2 loops on hook) twice. Skip hdc **behind** FPdc.

Row 3: Ch 2, turn; hdc in next hdc, ★ † skip next 2 hdc, work FPdc around hdc one row **below** next 2 hdc, working in **front** of FPdc just made (*Fig. 3a, page 59*), work FPdc around hdc one row **below** each skipped hdc †, hdc in next 4 hdc; repeat from ★ once **more**, then repeat from † to † once, hdc in last 2 hdc.

Row 5: Ch 2, turn; hdc in next hdc, ★ † skip next 2 FPdc, work FPdc around next 2 FPdc, working in **front** of FPdc just made, work FPdc around each skipped FPdc †, hdc in next 4 hdc; repeat from ★ once **more**, then repeat from † to † once, hdc in last 2 hdc.

Rows 7 and 9: Ch 2, turn; work FPdc around next 2 FPdc, (hdc in next 2 hdc, work FPdc next 2 FPdc) across to last hdc, hdc in last hdc.

Row 11: Ch 2, turn; hdc in next hdc, work FPdc around next 4 FPdc, (hdc in next 4 hdc, work FPdc around next 4 FPdc) twice, hdc in last 2 hdc.

Rows 13 and 15: Ch 2, turn; hdc in next hdc, ★ † skip next 2 FPdc, work FPdc around next 2 FPdc, working in **front** of FPdc just made, work FPdc around each skipped FPdc †, hdc in next 4 hdc; repeat from ★ once **more**, then repeat from † to † once, hdc in last 2 hdc.

Repeat Rows 8-15 until piece measures 7" (18 cm) from beginning ch; do **not** finish off, mark last row as **bottom** edge.

Work Edging (*see Finishing, page 10*).

46 bobble BRAID

Ch 24.

Row 1 (Right side)**:** Sc in second ch from hook and in each ch across: 23 sc.

Note: Loop a short piece of yarn around any stitch to mark Row 1 as **right** side and **bottom** edge.

Row 2 AND ALL WRONG SIDE ROWS: Ch 1, turn; sc in each st across.

To work Front Post double crochet (abbreviated FPdc), YO, insert hook from **front** to **back** around post of st indicated (*Fig. 1, page 59*), YO and pull up a loop, (YO and draw through 2 loops on hook) twice. Skip sc **behind** FPdc.

To work Popcorn (uses one sc), 5 sc in next sc, drop loop from hook, insert hook in first sc of 5-sc group, hook dropped loop and draw through st. Ch 1 to close.

Row 3: Ch 1, turn; sc in first sc, work FPdc around sc one row **below** next sc, sc in next sc, ★ work Popcorn, sc in next 7 sc, work FPdc around sc one row **below** next sc, sc in next sc; repeat from ★ once **more**.

Row 5: Ch 1, turn; sc in first sc, work FPdc around next FPdc, ★ sc in next 3 sc, work FPdc around top of next Popcorn, sc in next 3 sc, work Popcorn, sc in next sc, work FPdc around next FPdc; repeat from ★ once **more**, sc in last sc.

Row 7: Ch 1, turn; sc in first sc, work FPdc around next FPdc, ★ sc in next 4 sc, work FPdc around next FPdc, sc in next sc, work FPdc around top of next Popcorn, sc in next 2 sc, work FPdc around next FPdc; repeat from ★ once **more**, sc in last sc.

Row 9: Ch 1, turn; sc in first sc, work FPdc around next FPdc, sc in next sc, ★ work Popcorn, sc in next 3 sc, skip next FPdc, work FPdc around next FPdc, working in **front** of FPdc just made (*Fig. 3a, page 59*), work FPdc in around skipped FPdc, sc in next 2 sc, work FPdc around next FPdc, sc in next sc; repeat from ★ once **more**.

Row 11: Ch 1, turn; sc in first sc, work FPdc around next FPdc, ★ sc in next 3 sc, work FPdc around top of next Popcorn, skip next FPdc, work FPdc around next FPdc, sc in next 2 sc, work Popcorn, sc in next sc, work FPdc around next FPdc; repeat from ★ once **more**, sc in last sc.

Repeat Rows 6-11 until piece measures 7" (18 cm) from beginning ch; do **not** finish off.

Work Edging (*see Finishing, page 10*).

bobbled CHEVRONS

Ch 26.

Row 1 (Right side)**:** Sc in second ch from hook and in each ch across: 25 sc.

Note: Loop a short piece of yarn around any stitch to mark Row 1 as **right** side and **bottom** edge.

Row 2: Ch 1, turn; sc in each st across.

To work Front Post double crochet (abbreviated FPdc), YO, insert hook from **front** to **back** around post of st indicated *(Fig. 1, page 59)*, YO and pull up a loop, (YO and draw through 2 loops on hook) twice. Skip sc **behind** FPdc.

Row 3: Ch 1, turn; sc in first 4 sc, † skip next sc, work FPdc around sc one row **below** next 2 sc, sc in next sc, work FPdc around same st as last FPdc made, work FPdc around sc one row **below** next sc †, sc in next 7 sc, repeat from † to † once, sc in last 4 sc.

To work Popcorn (uses one st), working in **or** around post of st indicated *(Fig. 1, page 59)*, work 5 sc, drop loop from hook, insert hook in first sc of 5-sc group, hook dropped loop and draw through st. Ch 1 to close.

Row 5: Ch 1, turn; sc in first 3 sc, † work FPdc around next 2 FPdc, sc in next sc, work Popcorn in next sc, sc in next sc, work FPdc around next 2 FPdc †, sc in next 5 sc, repeat from † to † once, sc in last 3 sc.

Row 7: Ch 1, turn; sc in first 2 sc, † work FPdc around next 2 FPdc, sc in next 5 sc, work FPdc around next 2 FPdc †, sc in next 3 sc, repeat from † to † once, sc in last 2 sc.

Row 9: Ch 1, turn; sc in first 2 sc, † work Popcorn around next FPdc, sc in next 7 sc, skip next FPdc, work Popcorn around next FPdc †, sc in next 3 sc, repeat from † to † once, sc in last 2 sc.

Repeat Rows 2-7 until piece measures 7" (18 cm) from beginning ch; do **not** finish off.

Work Edging *(see Finishing, page 10).*

DOUBLE waves & bobbles

Ch 26.

Row 1 (Right side)**:** Sc in second ch from hook and in each ch across: 25 sc.

Note: Loop a short piece of yarn around any stitch to mark Row 1 as **right** side and **bottom** edge.

Row 2 AND ALL WRONG SIDE ROWS: Ch 1, turn; sc in each st across.

To work Front Post double crochet (abbreviated FPdc), YO, insert hook from **front** to **back** around post of st indicated *(Fig. 1, page 59)*, YO and pull up a loop, (YO and draw through 2 loops on hook) twice. Skip sc **behind** FPdc unless otherwise instructed.

To work Popcorn (uses one sc), 5 sc in next sc, drop loop from hook, insert hook in first sc of 5-sc group, hook dropped loop and draw through st. Ch 1 to close.

Row 3: Ch 1, turn; sc in first 4 sc, work Popcorn, sc in next 5 sc, skip next sc, work FPdc around sc one row **below** next 2 sc, sc in next sc, work FPdc around same st as last FPdc, work FPdc around sc one row **below** next sc, sc in next 5 sc, work Popcorn, sc in last 4 sc.

Row 5: Ch 1, turn; sc in first 4 sc, work Popcorn, sc in next 4 sc, work FPdc around next 2 FPdc, sc in next sc, work Popcorn, sc in next sc, work FPdc around next 2 FPdc, sc in next 4 sc, work Popcorn, sc in last 4 sc.

Row 7: Ch 1, turn; sc in first 4 sc, work Popcorn, sc in next 6 sc, work FPdc around next 4 FPdc, skip next 3 sc **behind** FPdc, sc in next 6 sc, work Popcorn, sc in last 4 sc: 26 sts.

Row 9: Ch 1, turn; sc in first 4 sc, work Popcorn, sc in next 5 sc, work FPdc around next 2 FPdc, sc in next sc, work FPdc around next 2 FPdc, skip next 3 sc **behind** FPdc, sc in next 5 sc, work Popcorn, sc in last 4 sc: 25 sts.

Row 11: Ch 1 turn, sc in first 4 sc, work Popcorn, sc in next 4 sc, work FPdc around next 2 FPdc, sc in next 3 sc, work FPdc around next 2 FPdc, sc in next 4 sc, work Popcorn, sc in last 4 sc.

Row 13: Ch 1, turn; sc in first 4 sc, work Popcorn, sc in next 3 sc, work FPdc around next 2 FPdc, sc in next 5 sc, work FPdc around next 2 FPdc, sc in next 3 sc, work Popcorn, sc in last 4 sc.

Row 15: Ch 1, turn; sc in first 4 sc, work Popcorn, sc in next 2 sc, work FPdc around next 2 FPdc, sc in next 7 sc, work FPdc around next 2 FPdc, sc in next 2 sc, work Popcorn, sc in last 4 sc.

Row 17: Ch 1, turn; sc in first 4 sc, work Popcorn, sc in next 3 sc, work FPdc around next 2 FPdc, sc in next 5 sc, work FPdc around next 2 FPdc, sc in next 3 sc, work Popcorn, sc in last 4 sc.

Row 19: Ch 1, turn; sc in first 4 sc, work Popcorn, sc in next 4 sc, work FPdc around next 2 FPdc, sc in next 3 sc, work FPdc around next 2 FPdc, sc in next 4 sc, work Popcorn, sc in last 4 sc.

Row 21: Ch 1, turn; sc in first 4 sc, work Popcorn, sc in next 5 sc, work FPdc around next 2 FPdc, sc in next sc, work FPdc around next 2 FPdc, sc in next 5 sc, work Popcorn, sc in last 4 sc.

To decrease (uses 2 FPdc), YO, insert hook from **front** to **back** around post of first skipped FPdc (*Fig. 1, page 59*), YO and pull up a loop, YO and draw through 2 loops on hook, YO, insert hook from **front** to **back** around post of next skipped FPdc, YO and pull up a loop, YO and draw through 2 loops on hook, YO and draw through all 3 loops on hook. Skip sc **behind** decrease.

Row 23: Ch 1, turn; sc in first 4 sc, work Popcorn, sc in next 6 sc, skip next 2 FPdc, work FPdc around next 2 FPdc, working in **front** of FPdc just made (*Fig. 3a, page 59*), work decrease, sc in next 6 sc, work Popcorn, sc in last 4 sc.

Row 25: Ch 1, turn; sc in first 4 sc, work Popcorn, sc in next 6 sc, work FPdc around next FPdc, work 2 FPdc around next FPdc, work FPdc around next decrease, sc in next 6 sc, work Popcorn, sc in last 4 sc: 26 sts.

Row 27: Ch 1, turn; sc in first 4 sc, work Popcorn, sc in next 5 sc, skip next 2 FPdc, work FPdc around next 2 FPdc, sc in next sc, working in **front** of last FPdc made, work FPdc around each skipped FPdc, skip next 3 sc **behind** FPdc, sc in next 5 sc, work Popcorn, sc in last 4 sc: 25 sts.

Row 29: Ch 1, turn; sc in first 4 sc, work Popcorn, sc in next 4 sc, work FPdc around next 2 FPdc, sc in next sc, work Popcorn, sc in next sc, work FPdc around next 2 FPdc, sc in next 4 sc, work Popcorn, sc in last 4 sc; do **not** finish off.

Work Edging (*see Finishing, page 10*).

49 TRIPLE bobble chevrons

Ch 25.

Row 1 (Right side)**:** Hdc in third ch from hook (2 skipped chs count as first hdc) and in each ch across: 24 hdc.

Note: Loop a short piece of yarn around any stitch to mark Row 1 as **right** side and **bottom** edge.

Row 2 AND ALL WRONG SIDE ROWS: Ch 2 (counts as first hdc, now and throughout), turn; hdc in next st and in each st across.

To work Popcorn (uses one hdc), 5 hdc in next hdc, drop loop from hook, insert hook in first hdc of 5-hdc group, hook dropped loop and draw through st. Ch 1 to close.

Row 3: Ch 2, turn; hdc in next 5 hdc, work Popcorn, hdc in next 10 hdc, work Popcorn, hdc in last 6 hdc.

To work Front Post double crochet (abbreviated FPdc), YO, insert hook from **front** to **back** around post of st indicated (*Fig. 1, page 59*), YO and pull up a loop even with st on hook, (YO and draw through 2 loops on hook) twice. Skip hdc **behind** FPdc.

Row 5: Ch 2, turn; hdc in next 4 hdc, † work Popcorn, work FPdc around top of next Popcorn, work Popcorn †, hdc in next 8 hdc, repeat from † to † once, hdc in last 5 hdc.

Row 7: Ch 2, turn; hdc in next 3 hdc, † work FPdc around top of next Popcorn, hdc in next hdc, work FPdc around next FPdc, hdc in next hdc, work FPdc around top of next Popcorn †, hdc in next 6 hdc, repeat from † to † once, hdc in last 4 hdc.

Row 9: Ch 2, turn; hdc in next 2 hdc, † work FPdc around next FPdc, (hdc in next 2 hdc, work FPdc around next FPdc) twice †, hdc in next 4 hdc, repeat from † to † once, hdc in last 3 hdc.

Row 11: Ch 2, turn; hdc in next hdc, ★ work FPdc around next FPdc, hdc in next 7 hdc, work FPdc around next FPdc, hdc in next 2 hdc; repeat from ★ once **more**.

Repeat Rows 2-11 until piece measures 7" (18 cm) from beginning ch; do **not** finish off.

Work Edging (*see Finishing, page 10*).

50 corded DIAMOND

Ch 26.

Row 1 (Right side)**:** Sc in second ch from hook and in each ch across: 25 sc.

Note: Loop a short piece of yarn around any stitch to mark Row 1 as **right** side and **bottom** edge.

Row 2 AND ALL WRONG SIDE ROWS: Ch 1, turn; sc in each st across.

To work Front Post double crochet (abbreviated FPdc), YO, insert hook from **front** to **back** around post of st indicated *(Fig. 1, page 59)*, YO and pull up a loop, (YO and draw through 2 loops on hook) twice. Skip sc **behind** FPdc.

Row 3: Ch 1, turn; sc in first 11 sc, skip next sc, work 3 FPdc around sc one row **below** next sc, sc in last 11 sc.

Row 5: Ch 1, turn; sc in first 10 sc, work FPdc around next FPdc, (sc in next sc, work FPdc around next FPdc) twice, sc in last 10 sc.

Row 7: Ch 1, turn; sc in first 9 sc, work FPdc around next FPdc, (sc in next 2 sc, work FPdc around next FPdc) twice, sc in last 9 sc.

Row 9: Ch 1, turn; sc in first 8 sc, work FPdc around next FPdc, ★ sc in next sc, work FPdc around sc one row **below** next sc, sc in next sc, work FPdc around next FPdc; repeat from ★ once **more**, sc in last 8 sc.

Row 11: Ch 1, turn; sc in first 7 sc, work FPdc around next FPdc, sc in next 2 sc, work FPdc around next FPdc, (sc in next sc, work FPdc around next FPdc) twice, sc in next 2 sc, work FPdc around next FPdc, sc in last 7 sc.

Row 13: Ch 1, turn; sc in first 6 sc, work FPdc around next FPdc, sc in next sc, work FPdc around sc one row **below** next sc, sc in next sc, (work FPdc around next FPdc, sc in next sc) 3 times, work FPdc around sc one row **below** next sc, sc in next sc, work FPdc around next FPdc, sc in last 6 sc.

Row 15: Ch 1, turn; sc in first 7 sc, work FPdc around next 2 FPdc, sc in next sc, (work FPdc around next FPdc, sc in next sc) 3 times, work FPdc around next 2 FPdc, sc in last 7 sc.

Row 17: Ch 1, turn; sc in first 8 sc, work FPdc around next FPdc, (sc in next sc, work FPdc around next FPdc) 4 times, sc in last 8 sc.

Row 19: Ch 1, turn; sc in first 9 sc, work FPdc around next 2 FPdc, sc in next sc, work FPdc around next FPdc, sc in next sc, work FPdc around next 2 FPdc, sc in last 9 sc.

Row 21: Ch 1, turn; sc in first 10 sc, work FPdc around next FPdc, (sc in next sc, work FPdc around next FPdc) twice, sc in last 10 sc.

Row 23: Ch 1, turn; sc in first 11 sc, work FPdc around next 3 FPdc, sc in last 11 sc.

To work Front Post decrease (abbreviated FP decrease), YO, insert hook from **front** to **back** around first FPdc, YO and pull up a loop, YO and draw through 2 loops on hook, ★ YO, insert hook from **front** to **back** around **next** FPdc, YO and pull up a loop, YO and draw through 2 loops on hook; repeat from ★ once **more**, YO and draw through all 4 loops on hook. Skip sc **behind** FP decrease.

Row 25: Ch 1, turn; sc in first 12 sc, work FP decrease, sc in last 12 sc.

Row 27: Ch 1, turn; sc in first 11 sc, work 3 FPdc around top of FP decrease, sc in last 11 sc.

Row 29: Ch 1, turn; sc in first 10 sc, work FPdc around next FPdc, (sc in next sc, work FPdc around next FPdc) twice, sc in last 10 sc; do **not** finish off.

Work Edging *(see Finishing, page 10).*

51 hollow OAK

Ch 26.

Row 1: Sc in second ch from hook and in each ch across: 25 sc.

To work Popcorn (uses one sc), 5 sc in next sc, drop loop from hook, insert hook in first sc of 5-sc group, hook dropped loop and draw through st. Ch 1 to close.

Row 2 (Right side)**:** Ch 1, turn; sc in first 12 sc, work Popcorn, sc in last 12 sc.

Note: Loop a short piece of yarn around any stitch to mark Row 2 as **right** side and **bottom** edge.

Row 3 AND ALL WRONG SIDE ROWS: Ch 1, turn; sc in each st across.

Row 4: Ch 1, turn; sc in first 10 sc, work Popcorn, sc in next 3 sc, work Popcorn, sc in last 10 sc.

To work Front Post double crochet (abbreviated FPdc), YO, insert hook from **front** to **back** around post of st indicated *(Fig. 1, page 59)*, YO and pull up a loop, (YO and draw through 2 loops on hook) twice. Skip sc **behind** FPdc.

Row 6: Ch 1, turn; sc in first 9 sc, work FPdc around top of next Popcorn, skip next sc, work FPdc around sc one row **below** next sc, sc in next sc, work Popcorn, sc in next sc, work FPdc around sc one row **below** last sc worked into, work FPdc around top of next Popcorn, sc in last 9 sc.

Row 8: Ch 1, turn; sc in first 8 sc, work FPdc around next 2 FPdc, sc in next 5 sc, work FPdc around next 2 FPdc, sc in last 8 sc.

Rows 10 and 12: Ch 1, turn; sc in first 7 sc, (work FPdc around next 2 FPdc, sc in next 7 sc) twice.

Row 14: Ch 1, turn; sc in first 8 sc, work FPdc around next 2 FPdc, sc in next 5 sc, work FPdc around next 2 FPdc, sc in last 8 sc.

Row 16: Ch 1, turn; sc in first 9 sc, work FPdc around next 2 FPdc, sc in next sc, work Popcorn, sc in next sc, work FPdc around next 2 FPdc, sc in last 9 sc.

Repeat Rows 3-16 until piece measures 7" (18 cm) from beginning ch; do **not** finish off.

Work Edging *(see Finishing, page 10)*.

52 mini DIAMOND RIB

Ch 25.

Row 1 (Right side)**:** Sc in second ch from hook and in each ch across: 24 sc.

Note: Loop a short piece of yarn around any stitch to mark Row 1 as **right** side and **bottom** edge.

Row 2 AND ALL WRONG SIDE ROWS: Ch 1, turn; sc in each st across.

To work Front Post double crochet (abbreviated FPdc), YO, insert hook from **front** to **back** around post of st indicated *(Fig. 1, page 59)*, YO and pull up a loop, (YO and draw through 2 loops on hook) twice. Skip sc **behind** FPdc.

Row 3: Ch 1, turn; sc in first sc, ★ † work FPdc around sc one row **below** next 4 sc, sc in next sc †, skip next sc, work FPdc around sc one row **below** next sc, sc in next sc, work FPdc around same st as last FPdc made, sc in next sc; repeat from ★ once **more**, then repeat from † to † once.

To work Cluster (uses next 2 FPdc), ★ YO, insert hook from **front** to **back** around **next** FPdc, YO and pull up a loop, YO and draw through 2 loops on hook; repeat from ★ once **more**, YO and draw through all 3 loops on hook. Skip sc **behind** Cluster.

Row 5: Ch 1, turn; sc in first sc, work FPdc around next 4 FPdc, ★ sc in next 2 sc, work Cluster, sc in next 2 sc, work FPdc around next 4 FPdc; repeat from ★ once **more**, sc in last sc.

Row 7: Ch 1, turn; sc in first sc, ★ † work FPdc around next 4 FPdc, sc in next sc †, work FPdc around top of next Cluster, sc in next sc, work FPdc around same st as last FPdc made, sc in next sc; repeat from ★ once **more**, then repeat from † to † once.

Repeat Rows 4-7 until piece measures 7" (18 cm) from beginning ch; do **not** finish off.

Work Edging *(see Finishing, page 10)*.

53 CABLED hearts

Ch 25.

Row 1 (Right side)**:** Sc in second ch from hook and in each ch across: 24 sc.

Note: Loop a short piece of yarn around any stitch to mark Row 1 as **right** side and **bottom** edge.

Row 2 AND ALL WRONG SIDE ROWS: Ch 1, turn; sc in each st across.

To work Front Post double crochet (abbreviated FPdc), YO, insert hook from **front** to **back** around post of st indicated *(Fig. 1, page 59)*, YO and pull up a loop, (YO and draw through 2 loops on hook) twice. Skip sc **behind** FPdc.

Row 3: Ch 1, turn; sc in first 5 sc, † skip next sc, work FPdc around sc one row **below** next sc, working in **front** of FPdc just made *(Fig. 3a, page 59)*, work FPdc around sc one row **below** skipped sc †, sc in next 10 sc, repeat from † to † once, sc in last 5 sc.

Row 5: Ch 1, turn; sc in first 4 sc, † work FPdc around next FPdc, sc in next 2 sc, work FPdc around next FPdc †, sc in next 8 sc, repeat from † to † once, sc in last 4 sc.

Row 7: Ch 1, turn; sc in first 3 sc, † work FPdc around next FPdc, sc in next 4 sc, work FPdc around next FPdc †, sc in next 6 sc, repeat from † to † once, sc in last 3 sc.

Row 9: Ch 1, turn; sc in first 2 sc, † work FPdc around next FPdc, sc in next 2 sc, skip next sc, work FPdc around sc one row **below** next sc, working in **front** of FPdc just made, work FPdc around sc one row **below** skipped sc, sc in next 2 sc, work FPdc around next FPdc †, sc in next 4 sc, repeat from † to † once, sc in last 2 sc.

Row 11: Ch 1, turn; sc in first sc, work FPdc around next FPdc, (sc in next 2 sc, work FPdc around next FPdc) across to last sc, sc in last sc.

Row 13: Ch 1, turn; sc in first sc, † work FPdc around next FPdc, sc in next sc, work FPdc around next FPdc †, sc in next 4 sc, repeat from † to † once, sc in next 2 sc, repeat from † to † once, sc in next 4 sc, repeat from † to † once, sc in last sc.

Row 15: Ch 1, turn; sc in first 3 sc, † skip next FPdc, work FPdc around next FPdc, working in **front** of FPdc just made, work FPdc around skipped FPdc †, sc in next 2 sc, repeat from † to † once, sc in next 6 sc, repeat from † to † once, sc in next 2 sc, repeat from † to † once, sc in last 3 sc.

Row 17: Ch 1, turn; sc in each sc across.

Repeat Rows 2-17 until piece measures 7" (18 cm) from beginning ch; do **not** finish off.

Work Edging *(see Finishing, page 10).*

Ch 26.

Row 1 (Right side)**:** Sc in second ch from hook and in each ch across: 25 sc.

Note: Loop a short piece of yarn around any stitch to mark Row 1 as **right** side and **bottom** edge.

Row 2 AND ALL WRONG SIDE ROWS: Ch 1, turn; sc in each st across.

To work Front Post double crochet (abbreviated FPdc), YO, insert hook from **front** to **back** around post of st indicated *(Fig. 1, page 59)*, YO and pull up a loop, (YO and draw through 2 loops on hook) twice. Skip sc **behind** FPdc.

Row 3: Ch 1, turn; sc in first 3 sc, ★ † work FPdc around sc one row **below** next 2 sc, sc in next sc, work FPdc around sc one row **below** next 2 sc †, sc in next 2 sc; repeat from ★ once **more**, then repeat from † to † once, sc in last 3 sc.

Row 5: Ch 1, turn; sc in first 2 sc, ★ † work FPdc around next 2 FPdc, sc in next sc, work FPdc around next 2 FPdc †, sc in next 2 sc; repeat from ★ once **more**, then repeat from † to † once, sc in last 4 sc.

Row 7: Ch 1, turn; sc in first sc, ★ † work FPdc around next 2 FPdc, sc in next sc, work FPdc around next 2 FPdc †, sc in next 2 sc; repeat from ★ once **more**, then repeat from † to † once, sc in last 5 sc.

To work Front Post treble crochet (abbreviated FPtr), YO twice, insert hook from **front** to **back** around post of st indicated *(Fig. 1, page 59)*, YO and pull up a loop, (YO and draw through 2 loops on hook) 3 times. Skip sc **behind** FPtr.

Row 9: Ch 1, turn; sc in first sc, ★ † skip next 2 FPdc, work FPtr around next 2 FPdc, sc in next sc, working in **front** of last FPtr made *(Fig. 3a, page 59)*, work FPtr around each skipped FPdc †, sc in next 2 sc; repeat from ★ once **more**, then repeat from † to † once, sc in last 5 sc.

Row 11: Ch 1, turn; sc in first 2 sc, ★ † work FPdc around next 2 FPtr, sc in next sc, work FPdc around next 2 FPtr †, sc in next 2 sc; repeat from ★ once **more**, then repeat from † to † once, sc in last 4 sc.

Row 13: Ch 1, turn; sc in first 3 sc, ★ † work FPdc around next 2 FPdc, sc in next sc, work FPdc around next 2 FPdc †, sc in next 2 sc; repeat from ★ once **more**, then repeat from † to † once, sc in last 3 sc.

Row 15: Ch 1, turn; sc in first 4 sc, ★ work FPdc around next 2 FPdc, sc in next sc, work FPdc around next 2 FPdc, sc in next 2 sc; repeat from ★ 2 times **more**.

Row 17: Ch 1, turn; sc in first 5 sc, ★ † work FPdc around next 2 FPdc, sc in next sc, work FPdc around next 2 FPdc †, sc in next 2 sc; repeat from ★ once **more**, then repeat from † to † once, sc in last sc.

Row 19: Ch 1, turn; sc in first 5 sc, ★ † skip next 2 FPdc, work FPtr around next 2 FPdc, sc in next sc, working in **front** of last FPtr made, work FPtr around each skipped FPdc †, sc in next 2 sc; repeat from ★ once **more**, then repeat from † to † once, sc in last sc.

Row 21: Ch 1, turn; sc in first 4 sc, ★ work FPdc around next 2 FPdc, sc in next sc, work FPdc around next 2 FPdc, sc in next 2 sc; repeat from ★ 2 times **more**.

Row 23: Ch 1, turn; sc in first 3 sc, ★ † work FPdc around next 2 FPdc, sc in next sc, work FPdc around next 2 FPdc †, sc in next 2 sc; repeat from ★ once **more**, then repeat from † to † once, sc in last 3 sc.

Rows 24-29: Repeat Rows 4-9; do **not** finish off.

Work Edging *(see Finishing, page 10)*.

 X'S & O'S

Ch 25.

Row 1 (Right side)**:** Sc in second ch from hook and in each ch across: 24 sc.

Note: Loop a short piece of yarn around any stitch to mark Row 1 as **right** side and **bottom** edge.

Row 2 AND ALL WRONG SIDE ROWS: Ch 1, turn; sc in each st across.

To work Front Post double crochet (abbreviated FPdc), YO, insert hook from **front** to **back** around post of st indicated *(Fig. 1, page 59)*, YO and pull up a loop, (YO and draw through 2 loops on hook) twice. Skip sc **behind** FPdc.

Row 3: Ch 1, turn; sc in first sc, work FPdc around sc one row **below** next 2 sc, (sc in next 2 sc, work FPdc around sc one row **below** next 2 sc) across to last sc, sc in last sc.

Row 5: Ch 1, turn; sc in first sc, work FPdc around next 2 FPdc, (sc in next 2 sc, work FPdc around next 2 FPdc) across to last sc, sc in last sc.

To work Front Post treble crochet (abbreviated FPtr), YO twice, insert hook from **front** to **back** around post of st indicated *(Fig. 1, page 59)*, YO and pull up a loop, (YO and draw through 2 loops on hook) 3 times. Skip sc **behind** FPtr.

Row 7: Ch 1, turn; sc in first sc, ★ † skip next 2 FPdc, work FPtr around next 2 FPdc, sc in next 2 sc, working in **front** of last FPtr made *(Fig. 3a, page 59)*, work FPtr around each skipped FPdc †, sc in next 2 sc; repeat from ★ once **more**, then repeat from † to † once, sc in last sc.

Row 9: Ch 1, turn; sc in first sc, work FPdc around next 2 FPtr, (sc in next 2 sc, work FPdc around next 2 FPtr) across to last sc, sc in last sc.

Row 11: Ch 1, turn; sc in first sc, work FPdc around next 2 FPdc, (sc in next 2 sc, work FPdc around next 2 FPdc) across to last sc, sc in last sc.

Row 13: Ch 1, turn; sc in first sc, ★ † skip next 3 sc, work 2 FPdc around sc one row **below** next sc, sc in third skipped sc and in next sc, working in **front** of last FPdc made, work 2 FPdc around sc 2 rows **below** first sc made †, sc in next 2 sc; repeat from ★ once **more**, then repeat from † to † once, sc in last sc.

Row 15: Ch 1, turn; sc in first sc, work FPdc around next 2 FPdc, (sc in next 2 sc, work FPdc around next 2 FPdc) across to last sc, sc in last sc.

Row 17: Ch 1, turn; sc in first sc, ★ † skip next 2 FPdc, work FPdc around next 2 FPdc, sc in next 2 sc, working in **front** of last FPdc made, work FPdc around each skipped FPdc †, sc in next 2 sc; repeat from ★ once **more**, then repeat from † to † once, sc in last sc.

Row 19: Ch 1, turn; sc in first sc, work FPdc around next 2 FPdc, (sc in next 2 sc, work FPdc around next 2 FPdc) across to last sc, sc in last sc.

Repeat Rows 4-19 until piece measures 7" (18 cm) from beginning ch; do **not** finish off.

Work Edging *(see Finishing, page 10)*.

56 fancy CHEVRON

Ch 25.

Row 1 (Right side)**:** Hdc in third ch from hook (2 skipped chs count as first hdc) and in each ch across: 24 hdc.

Note: Loop a short piece of yarn around any stitch to mark Row 1 as **right** side and **bottom** edge.

Row 2 AND ALL WRONG SIDE ROWS: Ch 2 (counts as first hdc, now and throughout), turn; hdc in next st and in each st across.

To work Front Post treble crochet (abbreviated FPtr), YO twice, insert hook from **front** to **back** around post of st indicated (*Fig. 1, page 59*), YO and pull up a loop, (YO and draw through 2 loops on hook) 3 times. Skip hdc **behind** FPtr.

Row 3: Ch 2, turn; hdc in next 8 hdc, skip next 4 hdc, work FPtr around hdc one row **below** next 2 hdc, sc in third and fourth skipped hdc, working in **front** of last FPtr made (*Fig. 3a, page 59*), work FPtr around hdc one row **below** first 2 skipped hdc, hdc in last 9 hdc.

To work Front Post double crochet (abbreviated FPdc), YO, insert hook from **front** to **back** around post of st indicated (*Fig. 1, page 59*), YO and pull up a loop even with st on hook, (YO and draw through 2 loops on hook) twice. Skip hdc **behind** FPdc unless otherwise insructed.

Row 5: Ch 2, turn; hdc in next 8 hdc, work FPdc around next 2 FPtr, sc in next 2 hdc, work FPdc around next 2 FPtr, hdc in last 9 hdc.

Row 7: Ch 2, turn; hdc in next 9 hdc, skip next 2 FPdc, work FPtr around next 2 FPdc, working in **front** of last FPtr made, work FPtr around each skipped FPdc, hdc in last 10 hdc.

Row 9: Ch 2, turn; hdc in next 8 hdc, work FPdc around next 2 FPtr, hdc in next 2 hdc, work FPdc around next 2 FPtr, hdc in last 9 hdc.

Row 11: Ch 2, turn; hdc in next 7 hdc, work FPdc around next 2 FPdc, hdc in next 4 hdc, work FPdc around next 2 FPdc, hdc in last 8 hdc.

Row 13: Ch 2, turn; (hdc in next 6 hdc, work FPdc around next 2 FPdc) twice, hdc in last 7 hdc.

To work Popcorn (uses one hdc), 5 hdc in next hdc, drop loop from hook, insert hook in first hdc of 5-hdc group, hook dropped loop and draw through st. Ch 1 to close.

Row 15: Ch 2, turn; hdc in next 4 hdc, work Popcorn, work FPdc around next 2 FPdc, hdc in next 8 hdc, work FPdc around next 2 FPdc, work Popcorn, hdc in last 5 hdc.

Row 17: Ch 2, turn; hdc in next 4 hdc, work FPdc around next 2 FPdc, hdc in next 3 hdc, skip next 3 hdc, work 2 FPtr around hdc one row **below** next hdc, sc in second and third skipped hdc, working in **front** of last FPtr made, work 2 FPtr around hdc one row **below** second skipped hdc, skip next hdc **behind** FPtr tr, hdc in next 3 hdc, work FPdc around next 2 FPdc, hdc in last 5 hdc: 26 sts.

Row 19: Ch 2, turn; hdc in next 9 hdc, skip next 2 FPdc, work FPtr around next 2 FPdc, working in **front** of last FPtr made, work FPtr around each skipped FPdc, skip next 6 hdc **behind** FPtr, hdc in last 10 hdc; do **not** finish off.

Work Edging (*see Finishing, page 10*).

57 triple CORDED CABLE

Ch 26.

Row 1 (Right side)**:** Hdc in third ch from hook (**2 skipped chs count as first hdc**) and in each ch across: 25 hdc.

Note: Loop a short piece of yarn around any stitch to mark Row 1 as **right** side and **bottom** edge.

Row 2 AND ALL WRONG SIDE ROWS: Ch 2 (**counts as first hdc, now and throughout**), turn; hdc in next st and in each st across.

To work Front Post treble crochet (abbreviated FPtr), YO twice, insert hook from **front** to **back** around post of st indicated (*Fig. 1, page 59*), YO and pull up a loop, (YO and draw through 2 loops on hook) 3 times. Skip hdc **behind** FPtr.

Row 3: Ch 2, turn; hdc in next 3 hdc, ★ skip next 2 hdc, work FPtr around hdc one row **below** next hdc, working in **front** of last FPtr made (*Fig. 3a, page 59*), work FPtr around hdc one row **below** each skipped hdc, hdc in next 4 hdc; repeat from ★ 2 times **more**.

Rows 5, 7, and 9: Ch 2, turn; hdc in next 2 hdc, ★ † work FPtr around next FPtr, (hdc in next hdc, work FPtr around next FPtr) twice †, hdc in next 2 hdc; repeat from ★ once **more**, then repeat from † to † once, hdc in last 3 hdc.

Rows 11 and 13: Ch 2, turn; hdc in next 3 hdc, ★ skip next 2 FPtr, work FPtr around next FPtr, working in **front** of last FPtr made, work FPtr around skipped FPtr, hdc in next 4 hdc; repeat from ★ 2 times **more**.

Repeat Rows 4-13 until piece measures 7" (18 cm) from beginning ch; do **not** finish off.

Work Edging (*see Finishing, page 10*).

58 bobbled Waves

Ch 24.

Row 1 (Right side)**:** Sc in second ch from hook and in each ch across: 23 sc.

Note: Loop a short piece of yarn around any stitch to mark Row 1 as **right** side.

Row 2 AND ALL WRONG SIDE ROWS: Ch 1, turn; sc in each st across.

To work Front Post double crochet (abbreviated FPdc), YO, insert hook from **front** to **back** around post of st indicated (*Fig. 1, page 59*), YO and pull up a loop, (YO and draw through 2 loops on hook) twice. Skip sc **behind** FPdc.

To work Popcorn (uses one sc), 5 sc in next sc, drop loop from hook, insert hook in first sc of 5-sc group, hook dropped loop and draw through st. Ch 1 to close.

Row 3: Ch 1, turn; sc in first 4 sc, ★ † work Popcorn, work FPdc around sc one row **below** next 2 sc †, sc in next 3 sc; repeat from ★ once **more**, then repeat from † to † once, sc in last 4 sc.

Row 5: Ch 1, turn; sc in first 4 sc, work FPdc around next 2 FPdc, (sc in next 4 sc, work FPdc around next 2 FPdc) twice, sc in last 5 sc.

Row 7: Ch 1, turn; sc in first 3 sc, work FPdc around next 2 FPdc, (sc in next 4 sc, work FPdc around next 2 FPdc) twice, sc in last 6 sc.

Row 9: Ch 1, turn; sc in first 2 sc, work FPdc around next 2 FPdc, (sc in next 4 sc, work FPdc around next 2 FPdc) twice, sc in last 7 sc.

Row 11: Ch 1, turn; sc in first sc, ★ † work FPdc around next 2 FPdc, work Popcorn †, sc in next 3 sc; repeat from ★ once **more**, then repeat from † to † once, sc in last 7 sc.

Row 13: Ch 1, turn; sc in first 2 sc, skip first FPdc, work FPdc around next FPdc, work FPdc around top of next Popcorn, ★ sc in next 4 sc, skip next FPdc, work FPdc around next FPdc, work FPdc around top of next Popcorn; repeat from ★ once **more**, sc in last 7 sc.

Row 15: Ch 1, turn; sc in first 3 sc, skip first FPdc, work FPdc around next FPdc, work FPdc around sc one row **below** next sc, ★ sc in next 4 sc, skip next FPdc, work FPdc around next FPdc, work FPdc around sc one row **below** next sc; repeat from ★ once **more**, sc in last 6 sc.

Row 17: Ch 1, turn; sc in first 4 sc, skip first FPdc, work FPdc around next FPdc, work FPdc around sc one row **below** next sc, ★ sc in next 4 sc, skip next FPdc, work FPdc around next FPdc, work FPdc around sc one row **below** next sc; repeat from ★ once **more**, sc in last 5 sc.

Row 19: Ch 1, turn; sc in first 4 sc, work Popcorn, work FPdc around next FPdc, work FPdc around sc one row **below** next sc, ★ sc in next 3 sc, work Popcorn, work FPdc around next FPdc, work FPdc around sc one row **below** next sc; repeat from ★ once **more**, sc in last 4 sc.

Repeat Rows 4-19 until piece measures 7" (18 cm) from beginning ch; do **not** finish off, mark last row as **bottom** edge.

Work Edging (*see Finishing, page 10*).

59 celtic BORDER

Ch 25.

Row 1 (Right side)**:** Hdc in third ch from hook (**2 skipped chs count as first hdc**) and in each ch across: 24 hdc.

Note: Loop a short piece of yarn around any stitch to mark Row 1 as **right** side and **bottom** edge.

Row 2 AND ALL WRONG SIDE ROWS: Ch 2 (**counts as first hdc, now and throughout**), turn; hdc in next st and in each st across.

To work Front Post treble crochet (abbreviated FPtr), YO twice, insert hook from **front** to **back** around post of st indicated (*Fig. 1, page 59*), YO and pull up a loop, (YO and draw through 2 loops on hook) 3 times. Skip hdc **behind** FPtr.

Row 3: Ch 2, turn; hdc in next 3 hdc, † skip next 2 hdc, work FPtr around hdc one row **below** next 2 hdc, working in **front** of FPtr just made (*Fig. 3a, page 59*), work FPtr around hdc one row **below** each skipped hdc †, hdc in next 8 hdc, repeat † to † once, hdc in last 4 hdc.

Row 5: Ch 2, turn; hdc in next 2 hdc, † work FPtr around next 2 FPtr, hdc in next 2 hdc, work FPtr around next 2 FPtr †, hdc in next 6 hdc, repeat from † to † once, hdc in last 3 hdc.

Row 7: Ch 2, turn; hdc in next 3 hdc, † skip next 2 FPtr, work FPtr around next 2 FPtr, working in **front** of FPtr just made, work FPtr around each skipped FPtr †, hdc in next 8 hdc, repeat from † to † once, hdc in last 4 hdc.

Row 9: Ch 2, turn; hdc in next 2 hdc, † work FPtr around next 2 FPtr, hdc in next 2 hdc, work FPtr around next 2 FPtr †, hdc in next 6 hdc, repeat from † to † once, hdc in last 3 hdc.

Row 11: Ch 2, turn; hdc in next hdc, work FPtr around next 2 FPtr, (hdc in next 4 hdc, work FPtr around next 2 FPtr) 3 times, hdc in last 2 hdc.

Row 13: Ch 2, turn; † work FPtr around next 2 FPtr, hdc in next 6 hdc, work FPtr around next 2 FPtr † hdc in next 2 hdc, repeat from † to † once, hdc in last hdc.

Row 15: Ch 2, turn; skip first FPtr, work FPtr around next FPtr, hdc in next 8 hdc, skip next 2 FPtr, work FPtr around next 2 FPtr, working in **front** of FPtr just made, work FPtr around each skipped FPtr, hdc in next 8 hdc, work FPtr around next FPtr, hdc in last hdc.

Row 17: Ch 2, turn; hdc in next 8 hdc, work FPtr around next 2 FPtr, hdc in next 2 hdc, work FPtr around next 2 FPtr, hdc in last 9 hdc.

Row 19: Ch 2, turn; hdc in next 9 hdc, skip next 2 FPtr, work FPtr around next 2 FPtr, working in **front** of FPtr just made, work FPtr around each skipped FPtr, hdc in last 10 hdc; do **not** finish off.

Work Edging (*see Finishing, page 10*).

 LANTERN

Ch 25.

Row 1 (Right side)**:** Hdc in third ch from hook **(2 skipped chs count as first hdc)** and in each ch across: 24 hdc.

Note: Loop a short piece of yarn around any stitch to mark Row 1 as **right** side and **bottom** edge.

Row 2 AND ALL WRONG SIDE ROWS: Ch 2 **(counts as first hdc, now and throughout),** turn; hdc in next st and in each st across.

To work Front Post double crochet (abbreviated FPdc), YO, insert hook from **front** to **back** around post of st indicated *(Fig. 1, page 59),* YO and pull up a loop even with st on hook, (YO and draw through 2 loops on hook) twice. Skip hdc **behind** FPdc.

Row 3: Ch 2, turn; hdc in next 10 hdc, work FPdc around hdc one row **below** next 2 hdc, hdc in last 11 hdc.

Row 5: Ch 2, turn; hdc in next 8 hdc, work 3 FPdc around each of next 2 FPdc, hdc in last 9 hdc.

Row 7: Ch 2, turn; hdc in next 6 hdc, (work FPdc around next FPdc, hdc in next hdc) twice, work FPdc around next 2 FPdc, (hdc in next hdc, work FPdc around next FPdc) twice, hdc in last 7 hdc.

Rows 9, 11, and 13: Ch 2, turn; hdc in next 4 hdc, (work FPdc around next FPdc, hdc in next 2 hdc) twice, work FPdc around next 2 FPdc, (hdc in next 2 hdc, work FPdc around next FPdc) twice, hdc in last 5 hdc.

Rows 15 and 17: Ch 2, turn; hdc in next 6 hdc, (work FPdc around next FPdc, hdc in next hdc) twice, work FPdc around next 2 FPdc, (hdc in next hdc, work FPdc around next FPdc) twice, hdc in last 7 hdc.

Row 19: Ch 2, turn; hdc in next 8 hdc, work FPdc around next 6 FPdc, hdc in last 9 hdc.

To decrease (uses 3 FPdc), ★ YO, insert hook from **front** to **back** around post of **next** FPdc, YO and pull up a loop, YO and draw through 2 loops on hook; repeat from ★ 2 times **more,** YO and draw through all 4 loops on hook. Skip hdc **behind** decrease.

Row 21: Ch 2, turn; hdc in next 10 hdc, decrease twice, hdc in last 11 hdc; do **not** finish off.

Work Edging *(see Finishing, page 10).*

 HONEYCOMB

Ch 27.

Row 1 (Right side)**:** Hdc in third ch from hook **(2 skipped chs count as first hdc)** and in each ch across: 26 hdc.

Note: Loop a short piece of yarn around any stitch to mark Row 1 as **right** side and **bottom** edge.

Row 2 AND ALL WRONG SIDE ROWS: Ch 2 **(counts as first hdc, now and throughout),** turn; hdc in next st and in each st across.

Row 3: Ch 2, turn; ★ skip next 2 hdc, dc in next 2 hdc, working **behind** dc just made *(Fig. 3b, page 59),* dc in each skipped hdc, skip next 2 hdc, dc in next 2 hdc, working in **front** of dc just made *(Fig. 3a, page 59),* dc in each skipped hdc; repeat from ★ across to last hdc, hdc in last hdc.

Row 5: Ch 2, turn; ★ skip next 2 hdc, dc in next 2 hdc, working in **front** of dc just made, dc in each skipped hdc, skip next 2 hdc, dc in next 2 hdc, working **behind** dc just made, dc in skipped hdc; repeat from ★ across to last hdc, hdc in last hdc.

Repeat Rows 2-5 until piece measures 7 " (18 cm) from beginning ch; do **not** finish off.

Work Edging *(see Finishing, page 10).*

wee DIAMONDS

Ch 26.

Row 1 (Right side)**:** Sc in second ch from hook and in each ch across: 25 sc.

Note: Loop a short piece of yarn around any stitch to mark Row 1 as **right** side and **bottom** edge.

Row 2 AND ALL WRONG SIDE ROWS: Ch 1, turn; sc in each st across.

To work Front Post double crochet (abbreviated FPdc), YO, insert hook from **front** to **back** around post of st indicated *(Fig. 1, page 59)*, YO and pull up a loop, (YO and draw through 2 loops on hook) twice. Skip sc **behind** FPdc.

Row 3: Ch 1, turn; sc in first sc, ★ skip next sc, work FPdc around sc one row **below** next sc, sc in next sc, work FPdc around **same** st as last FPdc made, sc in next sc; repeat from ★ across.

To work Cluster (uses next 2 FPdc), ★ YO, insert hook from **front** to **back** around **next** FPdc, YO and pull up a loop, YO and draw through 2 loops on hook; repeat from ★ once **more**, YO and draw through all 3 loops on hook. Skip sc **behind** Cluster.

Row 5: Ch 1, turn; sc in first 2 sc, work Cluster, (sc in next 3 sc, work Cluster) across to last 2 sc, sc in last 2 sc.

Row 7: Ch 1, turn; sc in first sc, ★ work FPdc around top of next Cluster, sc in next sc, work FPdc around **same** st as last FPdc made, sc in next sc; repeat from ★ across.

Repeat Rows 4-7 until piece measures 7" (18 cm) from beginning ch; do **not** finish off.

Work Edging *(see Finishing, page 10)*.

winter BERRIES

Ch 26.

Row 1 (Right side)**:** Sc in second ch from hook and in each ch across: 25 sc.

Note: Loop a short piece of yarn around any stitch to mark Row 1 as **right** side.

Row 2 AND ALL WRONG SIDE ROWS: Ch 1, turn; sc in each st across.

To work Cluster (uses one sc), ★ YO, insert hook in sc indicated, YO and pull up a loop, YO and draw through 2 loops on hook; repeat from ★ 5 times **more**, YO and draw through all 7 loops on hook.

Row 3: Ch 1, turn; sc in first 4 sc, work Cluster in next sc, (sc in next 3 sc, work Cluster in next sc) across to last 4 sc, sc in last 4 sc.

To work Front Post double crochet (abbreviated FPdc), YO, insert hook from **front** to **back** around post of st indicated *(Fig. 1, page 59)*, YO and pull up a loop, (YO and draw through 2 loops on hook) twice. Skip sc **behind** FPdc.

Row 5: Ch 1, turn; sc in first sc, ★ skip next 2 sc, work FPdc around sc 2 rows **below** next sc, sc in next sc, working in **front** of FPdc just made *(Fig. 3a, page 59)*, work FPdc around sc 2 rows **below** first skipped sc, sc in next sc; repeat from ★ across.

Repeat Rows 2-5 until piece measures 7" (18 cm) from beginning ch; do **not** finish off, mark last row as **bottom** edge.

Work Edging *(see Finishing, page 10)*.

bolster pillow

Shown on front cover.

■■■□ INTERMEDIATE

Finished Size: 14" long x 5" diameter
(35.5 cm x 12.5 cm)

MATERIALS

Medium Weight Yarn **[4]**
[3¹⁄₂ ounces, 166 yards
(100 grams, 152 meters) per skein]:
Brown - 1 skein
Tan - 1 skein
Lt Green - 1 skein
Green - 1 skein
Ecru - 1 skein
Crochet hooks, sizes G (4 mm) **and** H (5 mm) **or**
sizes needed for gauge
14" long x 5" diameter (35.5 cm x 12.5 cm)
Bolster pillow form
Yarn needle

GAUGE: With larger size hook and Ecru,
14 sc and 16 rows = 4" (10 cm)

Gauge Swatch: 4" (10 cm) square
With larger size hook and Ecru, ch 15.
Row 1: Sc in second ch from hook and in each
ch across: 14 sc.
Rows 2-16: Ch 1, turn; sc in each sc across.
Finish off.

STITCH GUIDE

FRONT POST DOUBLE CROCHET
(abbreviated FPdc)
YO, insert hook from **front** to **back** around post
of st indicated *(Fig. 1, page 59)*, YO and pull up
a loop, (YO and draw through 2 loops on hook)
twice. Skip st **behind** FPdc.
CLUSTER
★ YO, insert hook from **front** to **back** around post
of **next** FPdc *(Fig. 1, page 59)*, YO and pull up
a loop, YO and draw through 2 loops on hook;
repeat from ★ once **more**, YO and draw through all
3 loops on hook. Skip st **behind** Cluster.
POPCORN (uses one sc)
5 Sc in next sc, drop loop from hook, insert hook in
first sc of 5-sc group, hook dropped loop and draw
through st. Ch 1 to close.

STRIP #1

With larger size hook and Green, ch 6.

Row 1 (Right side): Sc in second ch from hook and in
each ch across: 5 sc.

Note: Loop a short piece of yarn around any stitch to
mark Row 1 as **right** side and **bottom** edge.

Row 2 AND ALL WRONG SIDE ROWS: Ch 1, turn;
sc in each st across.

Row 3: Ch 1, turn; sc in first sc, skip next sc, work FPdc
around sc one row **below** next sc, sc in next sc, work
FPdc around same st as first FPdc, sc in last sc.

Row 5: Ch 1, turn; sc in first 2 sc, work Cluster, sc in last
2 sc.

Row 7: Ch 1, turn; sc in first sc, skip next sc, work FPdc
around top of Cluster, sc in next sc, work FPdc around
same st as first FPdc, sc in last sc.

Rows 8-74: Repeat Rows 4-7, 16 times; then repeat
Rows 4-6 once **more**.

Finish off.

Change to smaller size hook.

First Side Trim: With **right** side facing and working in
end of rows, join Green with sc in last row *(see Joining
With Sc, page 59)*; work 71 sc evenly spaced across;
finish off: 72 sc.

Second Side Trim: With **right** side facing, smaller size
hook, and working in end of rows, join Green with sc in
first row; work 71 sc evenly spaced across; finish off: 72 sc.

STRIP #2

With larger size hook and Brown, ch 13.

Row 1: Sc in second ch from hook and in each ch
across: 12 sc.

Row 2 (Right side): Ch 1, turn; sc in each sc across.

Note: Mark Row 2 as **right** side and **bottom** edge.

Row 3 AND ALL WRONG SIDE ROWS: Ch 1, turn; sc in each st across.

Row 4: Ch 1, turn; sc in each sc across.

Row 6: Ch 1, turn; sc in first 5 sc, skip next sc, work FPdc around sc one row **below** next sc, working in **front** of FPdc just made (*Fig. 3a, page 59*), work FPdc around sc one row **below** skipped sc, sc in last 5 sc.

Row 8: Ch 1, turn; sc in first 4 sc, work FPdc around next FPdc, sc in next 2 sc, work FPdc around next FPdc, sc in last 4 sc.

Row 10: Ch 1, turn; sc in first 3 sc, work FPdc around next FPdc, sc in next 4 sc, work FPdc around next FPdc, sc in last 3 sc.

Row 12: Ch 1, turn; sc in first 2 sc, work FPdc around next FPdc, sc in next 2 sc, skip next sc, work FPdc around sc one row **below** next sc, working in **front** of FPdc just made, work FPdc around sc one row **below** skipped sc, sc in next 2 sc, work FPdc around next FPdc, sc in last 2 sc.

Row 14: Ch 1, turn; sc in first sc, work FPdc around next FPdc, (sc in next 2 sc, work FPdc around next FPdc) across to last sc, sc in last sc.

Row 16: Ch 1, turn; sc in first 2 sc, work FPdc around next 2 FPdc, sc in next 4 sc, work FPdc around next 2 FPdc, sc in last 2 sc.

Row 18: Ch 1, turn; sc in first 2 sc, † skip next FPdc, work FPdc around next FPdc, working in **front** of FPdc just made, work FPdc around skipped FPdc †, sc in next 4 sc, repeat from † to † once, sc in last 2 sc.

Row 20: Ch 1, turn; sc in each sc across.

Rows 21-66: Repeat Rows 5-20 twice; then repeat Rows 5-19 once **more**.

Rows 67-70: Ch 1, turn; sc in each sc across; at end of Row 70, do **not** finish off.

Change to smaller size hook.

First Side Trim: Ch 1, do **not** turn; working in end of rows, work 72 sc evenly spaced across; finish off.

Second Side Trim: With **right** side facing, smaller size hook, and working in end of rows, join Brown with sc in first row; work 71 sc evenly spaced across; finish off: 72 sc.

STRIP #3
With larger size hook and Ecru, ch 10.

Row 1 (Right side)**:** Sc in second ch from hook and in each ch across: 9 sc.

Note: Mark Row 1 as **right** side and **bottom** edge.

Row 2 AND ALL WRONG SIDE ROWS: Ch 1, turn; sc in each sc across.

Row 3: Ch 1, turn; sc in each sc across.

Row 5: Ch 1, turn; sc in first 3 sc, work Popcorn, work FPdc around sc one row **below** next 2 sc, sc in last 3 sc.

Row 7: Ch 1, turn; sc in first 3 sc, work FPdc around next 2 FPdc, sc in last 4 sc.

Row 9: Ch 1, turn; sc in first 2 sc, work FPdc around next 2 FPdc, sc in last 5 sc.

Row 11: Ch 1, turn; sc in first sc, work FPdc around next 2 FPdc, sc in last 6 sc.

Row 13: Ch 1, turn; sc in first sc, work FPdc around next 2 FPdc, work Popcorn, sc in last 5 sc.

Row 15: Ch 1, turn; sc in first 2 sc, work FPdc around next FPdc, work FPdc around top of next Popcorn, sc in last 5 sc.

Row 17: Ch 1, turn; sc in first 3 sc, work FPdc around next FPdc, work FPdc around sc one row **below** next sc, sc in last 3 sc.

Row 19: Ch 1, turn; sc in first 4 sc, work FPdc around next FPdc, work FPdc around sc one row **below** next sc, sc in last 3 sc.

Instructions continued on page 52.

Row 21: Ch 1, turn; sc in first 3 sc, work Popcorn, work FPdc around next 2 FPdc, sc in last 3 sc.

Rows 22-69: Repeat Rows 6-21, 3 times.

Rows 70-72: Ch 1, turn; sc in each sc across.

Finish off.

First Side Trim: With **right** side facing, smaller size hook, and working in end of rows, join Ecru with sc in last row; work 71 sc in evenly spaced across; finish off: 72 sc.

Second Side Trim: With **right** side facing, smaller size hook, and working in end of rows, join Ecru with sc in first row; work 71 sc in evenly spaced across; finish off: 72 sc.

STRIP #4
With larger size hook and Tan, ch 16.

Row 1: Sc in second ch from hook and in each ch across: 15 sc.

Row 2 (Right side): Ch 1, turn; sc in first 5 sc, work Popcorn, sc in next 3 sc, work Popcorn, sc in last 5 sc.

Note: Mark Row 2 as **right** side and **bottom** edge.

Row 3 AND ALL WRONG SIDE ROWS: Ch 1, turn; sc in each st across.

Row 4: Ch 1, turn; sc in first 4 sc, work FPdc around top of next Popcorn, work FPdc around sc one row **below** next sc, sc in next sc, work Popcorn, sc in next sc, work FPdc around sc one row **below** last sc worked into, work FPdc around top of next Popcorn, sc in last 4 sc.

Row 6: Ch 1, turn; sc in first 3 sc, work FPdc around next 2 FPdc, sc in next 5 sc, work FPdc around next 2 FPdc, sc in last 3 sc.

Row 8: Ch 1, turn; sc in first 2 sc, work FPdc around next 2 FPdc, sc in next 7 sc, work FPdc around next 2 FPdc, sc in last 2 sc.

Row 10: Ch 1, turn; sc in first 3 sc, work FPdc around next 2 FPdc, sc in next 5 sc, work FPdc around next 2 FPdc, sc in last 3 sc.

Row 12: Ch 1, turn; sc in first 4 sc, work FPdc around next 2 FPdc, sc in next sc, work Popcorn, sc in next sc, work FPdc around next 2 FPdc, sc in last 4 sc.

Row 14: Ch 1, turn; sc in first 5 sc, work Popcorn, sc in next 3 sc, work Popcorn, sc in last 5 sc.

Rows 15-73: Repeat Rows 3-14, 4 times; then repeat Rows 3-13 once **more**; do **not** finish off.

Change to smaller size hook.

First Side Trim: Ch 1, do **not** turn; working in end of rows, work 72 sc evenly spaced across; finish off.

Second Side Trim: With **right** side facing, smaller size hook, and working in end of rows, join Tan with sc in first row; work 71 sc evenly spaced across; finish off: 72 sc.

STRIP #5
With larger size hook and Lt Green, ch 9.

Row 1 (Right side): Sc in second ch from hook and in each ch across: 8 sc.

Note: Mark Row 1 as **right** side and **bottom** edge.

Row 2 AND ALL WRONG SIDE ROWS: Ch 1, turn; sc in each st across.

Row 3: Ch 1, turn; sc in first 2 sc, work FPdc around sc one row **below** next 4 sc, sc in last 2 sc.

Rows 5 and 7: Ch 1, turn; sc in first 2 sc, skip next 2 FPdc, work FPdc around next 2 FPdc, working in **front** of FPdc just made, work FPdc around each skipped FPdc, sc in last 2 sc.

Rows 9, 11, and 13: Ch 1, turn; sc in first 2 sc, work FPdc around next 4 FPdc, sc in last 2 sc.

Rows 14-73: Repeat Rows 2-13, 5 times; do **not** finish off.

Change to smaller size hook.

First Side Trim: Ch 1, do **not** turn; work 72 sc evenly spaced across end of rows; finish off.

Second Side Trim: With **right** side facing, smaller size hook, and working in end of rows, join Lt. Green with sc in first row; work 71 sc evenly spaced across; finish off: 72 sc.

END (Make 2)

Rnd 1 (Right side): With larger size hook and Brown, ch 2, 8 sc in second ch from hook; do **not** join, place marker *(see Markers, page 59)*.

Rnd 2: 2 Sc in each sc around: 16 sc.

Rnd 3: (2 Sc in next sc, sc in next sc) around: 24 sc.

Rnd 4: (2 Sc in next sc, sc in next 2 sc) around: 32 sc.

Rnd 5: (2 Sc in next sc, sc in next 3 sc) around: 40 sc.

Rnd 6: (2 Sc in next sc, sc in next 4 sc) around: 48 sc.

Rnd 7: Sc in each sc around.

Rnd 8: (2 Sc in next sc, sc in next 5 sc) around; slip st in next sc, finish off: 56 sc.

Rnd 9: With **right** side facing, join Ecru with sc in same st as slip st; sc in each sc around.

Rnd 10: (Sc in next sc, work Popcorn) around.

Rnd 11: Sc in next 2 sts, 2 sc in next st, sc in next 3 sts, ★ 2 sc in next st, (sc in next 2 sts, 2 sc in next st) twice, sc in next 3 sts; repeat from ★ around; slip st in next sc, finish off: 72 sc.

POPCORN

With larger size hook and Ecru, ch 2, 5 sc in second ch from hook, drop loop from hook, insert hook first sc of 5-sc group, hooked dropped loop and draw through st; finish off leaving a long end for sewing. Sew one Popcorn to **right** side of center on each End.

ASSEMBLY

Join Strips in numerical order.

With **right** sides facing, having bottom edges at same end and using smaller size hook, join Strips as follows: Working in inside loops of sc on Trim on both Strips *(Fig. A, page 57)*, join Ecru with slip st in first sc; holding yarn to back of work, slip st in next sc and in each sc across; finish off.

Fold piece in half. Matching last rows to beginning chs and using corresponding color yarn, whipstitch across to form a tube *(Fig. 4, page 59)*.

Trim: With **right** side facing, join Ecru with sc in first sc on Trim on either outer Strip; sc in each sc around; join with slip st to first sc; finish off.

Repeat Trim on opposite side.

With Ecru, whipstitch one End to tube. Insert pillow form. Whipstitch second End in same manner.

square pillow

Shown on front cover.

■■■□ INTERMEDIATE

Finished Size: 14" (35.5 cm) square

MATERIALS

Medium Weight Yarn 4

[3½ ounces, 166 yards
(100 grams, 152 meters) per skein]:
  Brown - 2 skeins
  Tan - 1 skein
  Lt Green - 1 skein
  Green - 1 skein
  Ecru - 1 skein
Crochet hooks, sizes G (4 mm) **and** H (5 mm) **or**
  sizes needed for gauge
14" (35.5 cm) Square pillow form
Yarn needle

GAUGE: With larger size hook and Ecru,
    14 sc and 16 rows = 4" (10 cm)

Gauge Swatch: 4" (10 cm) square
With larger size hook and Ecru, ch 15.
Row 1: Sc in second ch from hook and in each ch
across: 14 sc.
Rows 2-16: Ch 1, turn; sc in each sc across.
Finish off.

STITCH GUIDE

> **FRONT POST DOUBLE CROCHET**
>   *(abbreviated FPdc)*
> YO, insert hook from **front** to **back** around post
> of st indicated *(Fig. 1, page 59)*, YO and pull up
> a loop, (YO and draw through 2 loops on hook)
> twice. Skip st **behind** FPdc.
> **FRONT POST TREBLE CROCHET**
>   *(abbreviated FPtr)*
> YO twice, insert hook from **front** to **back** around
> post of st indicated *(Fig. 1, page 59)*, YO and pull
> up a loop, (YO and draw through 2 loops on hook)
> 3 times. Skip st **behind** FPtr.

> **DECREASE** (uses 4 FPdc)
> YO, insert hook from **front** to **back** around post of
> first FPdc of 4-FPdc group, YO and pull up a loop, YO
> and draw through 2 loops on hook, ★ YO, insert hook
> from **front** to **back** around post of **next** FPdc, YO and
> pull up a loop, YO and draw through 2 loops on hook;
> repeat from ★ 2 times **more**, YO and draw through all
> 5 loops on hook. Skip hdc **behind** decrease.
> **CLUSTER**
> ★ YO, insert hook from **front** to **back** around post
> of decrease one row **below**, YO and pull up a loop,
> YO and draw through 2 loops on hook; repeat from
> ★ 3 times **more**, YO and draw through all 5 loops
> on hook. Skip hdc **behind** Cluster.
> **FRONT POST POPCORN**
>   *(abbreviated FP Popcorn)* (uses one FPdc)
> 5 FPdc around post of next FPdc, drop loop from
> hook, insert hook in first dc of 5-FPdc group, hook
> dropped loop and draw through st. Ch 1 to close.
> **POPCORN** (uses one sc)
> 5 Sc in next sc, drop loop from hook, insert hook in
> first sc of 5-sc group, hook dropped loop and draw
> through st. Ch 1 to close.

BACK

With larger size hook and Brown, ch 45.

Row 1 (Right side)**:** Sc in second ch from hook and in
each ch across: 44 sc.

Note: Loop a short piece of yarn around any stitch to
mark Row 1 as **right** side.

Row 2 AND ALL WRONG SIDE ROWS: Ch 1, turn; sc
in each st across.

Row 3: Ch 1, turn; sc in first sc, work FPdc around sc
one row **below** next 2 sc, (sc in next 2 sc, work FPdc
around sc one row **below** next 2 sc) across to last sc, sc
in last sc.

Rows 5 and 7: Ch 1, turn; sc in first sc, work FPdc
around next 2 FPdc, (sc in next 2 sc, work FPdc around
next 2 FPdc) across to last sc, sc in last sc.

Row 9: Ch 1, turn; sc in first sc, work FPdc around next FPdc, sc in next sc, skip next FPdc, work FPdc around next FPdc, working in **front** of FPdc just made (*Fig. 3a, page 59*), work FPdc around skipped FPdc, ★ sc in next 2 sc, skip next FPdc, work FPdc around next FPdc, working in **front** of FPdc just made, work FPdc around skipped FPdc; repeat from ★ across to last 3 sc, sc in next sc, work FPdc around next FPdc, sc in last sc.

Row 11: Ch 1, turn; sc in first sc, work FPdc around next 2 FPdc, sc in next 2 sc, ★ skip next FPdc, work FPdc around next FPdc, working in **front** of FPdc just made, work FPdc around skipped FPdc, sc in next 2 sc; repeat from ★ across to last 3 sts, work FPdc around next 2 FPdc, sc in last sc.

Row 13: Ch 1, turn; sc in first sc, work FPdc around next 2 FPdc, (sc in next 2 sc, work FPdc around next 2 FPdc) across to last sc, sc in last sc.

Rows 14-53: Repeat Rows 2-13, 3 times; then repeat Rows 2-5 once; do **not** finish off.

Change to smaller size hook.

Edging: With **right** side facing, ch 1, (3 sc in corner, work 53 sc evenly spaced across to next corner) around; join with slip st to first sc, finish off: 224 sc.

FRONT
SQUARE #1
With Brown, ch 29.

Row 1 (Right side)**:** Sc in second ch from hook, ch 1, ★ skip next ch, sc in next 4 chs, ch 1; repeat from ★ across to last 2 chs, skip next ch, sc in last ch: 22 sc and 6 chs.

Note: Mark Row 1 as **right** side and **bottom** edge.

Row 2: Ch 1, turn; sc in each sc and in each ch across: 28 sc.

Row 3: Ch 1, turn; sc in first sc, working **around** next sc (*Fig. 2, page 59*), dc in ch-1 sp one row **below** next sc, ★ skip first 3 sc of next 4-sc group two rows **below**, work FPtr around next sc, ch 2, working in **front** of FPtr just made, work FPtr around first skipped sc, working **around** next sc, dc in ch-1 sp one row **below** next sc; repeat from ★ across to last sc, sc in last sc: 18 sts and 5 ch-2 sps.

Row 4: Ch 1, turn; sc in first 3 sts, ★ ch 2, skip next ch-2 sp, sc in next 3 sts; repeat from ★ across.

Row 5: Ch 1, turn; sc in first sc, work FPdc around dc one row **below** next sc, ★ work FPtr around next FPtr, ch 2, work FPtr around next FPtr, work FPdc around dc one row **below** next sc; repeat from ★ across to last sc, sc in last sc.

Row 6: Ch 1, turn; sc in first 3 sts, ★ ch 2, skip next ch-2 sp, sc in next 3 sts; repeat from ★ across.

Row 7: Ch 1, turn; sc in first sc, ★ work FPdc around next FPdc, skip next FPtr, work FPtr around next FPtr, working **behind** FPtr just made (*Fig. 3b, page 59*) and around ch-2, 2 sc in ch-2 sp 2 rows **below** next ch-2, working in **front** of last FPtr made, work FPtr around skipped FPtr, work FPdc around next FPdc; repeat from ★ across to last sc, sc in last sc.

Row 8: Ch 1, turn; sc in first 3 sts, ★ ch 2, skip next 2 sc, sc in next 3 sts; repeat from ★ across.

Repeat Rows 5-8 until piece measures 7" (18 cm) from beginning ch; do **not** finish off.

Change to smaller size hook.

Edging: With **right** side facing, ch 1, (3 sc in corner, work 25 sc evenly spaced across to next corner) around; join with slip st to first sc, finish off: 112 sc.

SQUARE #2
With larger size hook and Green, ch 26.

Row 1 (Right side)**:** Hdc in third ch from hook (**2 skipped chs count as first hdc**) and in each ch across: 25 hdc.

Note: Mark Row 1 as **right** side and **bottom** edge.

Row 2 AND ALL WRONG SIDE ROWS: Ch 2 (counts as first hdc, now and throughout), turn; hdc in next hdc and in each st across.

Row 3: Ch 2, turn; ★ hdc in next 2 hdc, work FPdc around hdc one row **below** next 2 hdc, hdc in next hdc, work FPdc around hdc one row **below** next 2 hdc; repeat from ★ 2 times **more**, hdc in last 3 hdc: 3 4-FPdc groups.

Instructions continued on page 56.

Row 5: Ch 2, turn; hdc in next 4 hdc, decrease, (hdc in next 6 hdc, decrease) twice, hdc in last 5 hdc.

Row 7: Ch 2, turn; hdc in next 4 hdc, work Cluster, (hdc in next 6 hdc, work Cluster) twice, hdc in last 5 hdc.

Row 9: Ch 2, turn; ★ hdc in next 2 hdc, work 2 FPdc around top of next Cluster, hdc in next hdc, work 2 FPdc around top of same Cluster; repeat from ★ 2 times **more**, hdc in last 3 hdc.

Rows 11 and 13: Ch 2, turn; ★ hdc in next 2 hdc, work FPdc around next 2 FPdc, hdc in next hdc, work FPdc around next 2 FPdc; repeat from ★ 2 times **more**, hdc in last 3 hdc.

Rows 15-21: Repeat Rows 4-11; do **not** finish off.

Change to smaller size hook.

Edging: With **right** side facing, ch 1, (3 sc in corner, work 25 sc evenly spaced across to next corner) around; join with slip st to first sc, finish off: 112 sc.

SQUARE #3
With larger size hook and Tan, ch 24.

Row 1 (Right side)**:** Hdc in third ch from hook (2 skipped chs count as first hdc) and in each ch across: 23 hdc.

Note: Mark Row 1 as **right** side and **bottom** edge.

Row 2 AND ALL EVEN NUMBERED ROWS THRU ROW 18: Ch 2, turn; hdc in next hdc and in each st across.

Row 3: Ch 2, turn; hdc in next 10 hdc, work FPdc around hdc one row **below** next hdc, hdc in last 11 hdc.

Row 5: Ch 2, turn; hdc in next 9 hdc, work FPdc around st one row **below** next 3 hdc, hdc in last 10 hdc.

Rows 7 and 9: Ch 2, turn; hdc in next 8 hdc, work FPdc around st one row **below** next 5 hdc, hdc in last 9 hdc.

Row 11: Ch 2, turn; hdc in next 8 hdc, skip next 3 FPdc, work FPtr around next 2 FPdc, working in **front** of FPtr just made, work FPtr around each skipped FPdc, hdc in last 9 hdc.

Row 13: Ch 2, turn; hdc in next 8 hdc, work FPdc around next 5 FPtr, hdc in last 9 hdc.

Row 15: Ch 2, turn; hdc in next 7 hdc, work FPdc around next FPdc, hdc in next hdc, work FPdc around next 3 FPdc, hdc in next hdc, work FPdc around next FPdc, hdc in last 8 hdc.

Row 17: Ch 2, turn; hdc in next 6 hdc, work FP Popcorn, (hdc in next hdc, work FPdc around next FPdc) 3 times, hdc in next hdc, work FP Popcorn, hdc in last 7 hdc.

Row 19: Ch 2, turn; hdc in next 8 hdc, work FP Popcorn, hdc in next hdc, work FPdc around next FPdc, hdc in next hdc, work FP Popcorn, hdc in last 9 hdc.

Row 20: Ch 1, turn sc in each st across.

Row 21: Ch 1, turn; sc in first 11 sc, work FP Popcorn, sc in last 11 sc; do **not** finish off.

Change to smaller size hook.

Edging: With **right** side facing, ch 1, (3 sc in corner, work 25 sc evenly spaced across to next corner) around; join with slip st to first sc, finish off: 112 sc.

SQUARE #4
With larger size hook and Lt Green, ch 24.

Row 1 (Right side)**:** Sc in second ch from hook and in each ch across: 23 sc.

Note: Mark Row 1 as **right** side and **bottom** edge.

Row 2 AND ALL WRONG SIDE ROWS: Ch 1, turn; sc in each st across.

Row 3: Ch 1, turn; sc in first sc, work FPdc around sc one row **below** next sc, sc in next sc, ★ work Popcorn, sc in next 7 sc, work FPdc around sc one row **below** next sc, sc in next sc; repeat from ★ once **more**.

Row 5: Ch 1, turn; sc in first sc, work FPdc around next FPdc, ★ sc in next 3 sc, FPdc around top of next Popcorn, sc in next 3 sc, work Popcorn in next sc, sc in next sc, work FPdc around next FPdc; repeat from ★ once **more**, sc in last sc.

Row 7: Ch 1, turn; sc in first sc, work FPdc around next FPdc, ★ sc in next 4 sc, work FPdc around next FPdc, sc in next sc, work FPdc around top of next Popcorn, sc in next 2 sc, work FPdc around next FPdc; repeat from ★ once **more**, sc in last sc.

Row 9: Ch 1, turn; sc in first sc, work FPdc around next FPdc, sc in next sc, ★ work Popcorn, sc in next 3 sc, work FPdc around next 2 FPdc, sc in next 2 sc, work FPdc around next FPdc, sc in next sc; repeat from ★ once **more**.

Row 11: Ch 1, turn; sc in first sc, work FPdc around next FPdc, ★ sc in next 3 sc, work FPdc around top of next Popcorn, skip next FPdc, work FPdc around next FPdc, sc in next 2 sc, work Popcorn, sc in next sc, work FPdc around next FPdc; repeat from ★ once **more**, sc in last sc.

Row 13: Ch 1, turn; sc in first sc, work FPdc around next FPdc, ★ sc in next 4 sc, work FPdc around next FPdc, sc in next sc, work FPdc around top of next Popcorn, sc in next 2 sc, work FPdc around next FPdc; repeat from ★ once **more**, sc in last sc.

Rows 14-27: Repeat Rows 8-13 twice, then repeat Rows 8 and 9 once **more**; do **not** finish off.

Change to smaller size hook.

Edging: With **right** side facing, ch 1, (3 sc in corner, work 25 sc evenly spaced across to next corner) around; join with slip st to first sc, finish off: 112 sc.

FINISHING
JOINING
Using photo as a guide for placement, holding two Squares side by side and working through **inside** loops, keeping Ecru to **wrong** side of both pieces, insert hook in center sc of 3-sc group *(Fig. A)*, YO and pull through sts, ★ insert hook in next sc, YO and pull through sts and loop on hook; repeat from ★ across; finish off.

Fig. A

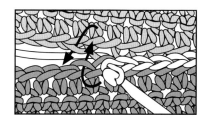

Repeat with remaining two Squares.
Join strips in same manner to form Front.

EDGING
With **right** side facing and using smaller size hook, join Ecru with sc in center sc of any corner 3-sc group; 2 sc in same st, ★ † work 53 sc evenly spaced across to center sc of next corner 3-sc group †, 3 sc in center sc; repeat from ★ once **more**, then repeat from † to † once; join with slip to first sc, finish off: 224 sc.

With **wrong** sides of Front and Back together, whipstitch pieces together using Ecru *(Fig. 4, page 59)*, inserting pillow form before closing.

TASSEL (Make 4)
Cut piece of cardboard 3" (7.5 cm) wide x 5" (12.5 cm) long. Wind a double strand of Ecru yarn around the cardboard approximately 38 times. Cut an 18" (45.5 cm) length of yarn and insert it under all of the strands at the top of the cardboard; pull up **tightly** and tie securely. Leave the yarn ends long enough to attach the tassel. Cut the yarn at the opposite end of the cardboard and then remove it *(Fig. B)*. Cut a 6" (15 cm) length of yarn and wrap it **tightly** around the tassel twice, 1" (2.5 cm) below the top; tie securely *(Fig. C)*. Trim ends.

Fig. B

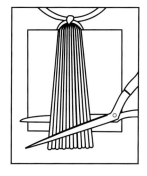

Fig. C

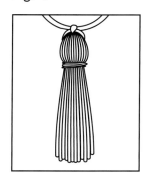

Attach one tassel to each corner.

general instructions

ABBREVIATIONS

ch(s)	chain(s)
cm	centimeters
dc	double crochet(s)
FP	front post
FPdc	Front Post double crochet(s)
FPdtr	Front Post double treble crochet(s)
FPtr	Front Post treble crochet(s)
FPtr tr	Front Post triple treble crochet(s)
hdc	half double crochet(s)
mm	millimeters
Rnd(s)	Round(s)
sc	single crochet(s)
sp(s)	space(s)
st(s)	stitch(es)
YO	yarn over

★ — work instructions following ★ as many **more** times as indicated in addition to the first time.

† to † — work all instructions from first † to second † as many times as specified.

( ) or [ ] — work enclosed instructions **as many** times as specified by the number immediately following **or** work all enclosed instructions in the stitch or space indicated **or** contains explanatory remarks.

colon (:) — the number(s) given after a colon at the end of a row or round denote(s) the number of stitches you should have on that row or round.

CROCHET TERMINOLOGY

UNITED STATES		INTERNATIONAL
slip stitch (slip st)	=	single crochet (sc)
single crochet (sc)	=	double crochet (dc)
half double crochet (hdc)	=	half treble crochet (htr)
double crochet (dc)	=	treble crochet (tr)
treble crochet (tr)	=	double treble crochet (dtr)
double treble crochet (dtr)	=	triple treble crochet (ttr)
triple treble crochet (tr tr)	=	quadruple treble crochet (qtr)
skip	=	miss

GAUGE

Exact gauge is **essential** for proper size. Before beginning your project, make the sample swatch given in the individual instructions in the yarn and hook specified. After completing the swatch, measure it, counting your stitches and rows carefully. If your swatch is larger or smaller than specified, **make another, changing hook size to get the correct gauge**. Keep trying until you find the size hook that will give you the specified gauge.

HINTS

As in all crocheted pieces, good finishing techniques make a big difference in the quality of the piece. Make a habit of taking care of loose ends as you work. Thread a yarn needle with the yarn end. With **wrong** side facing, weave the needle through several stitches, then reverse the direction and weave it back through several stitches. When ends are secure, clip them off close to work.

Yarn Weight Symbol & Names	SUPER FINE 1	FINE 2	LIGHT 3	MEDIUM 4	BULKY 5	SUPER BULKY 6
Type of Yarns in Category	Sock, Fingering Baby	Sport, Baby	DK, Light Worsted	Worsted, Afghan, Aran	Chunky, Craft, Rug	Bulky, Roving
Crochet Gauge Ranges in Single Crochet to 4" (10 cm)	21-32 sts	16-20 sts	12-17 sts	11-14 sts	8-11 sts	5-9 sts
Advised Hook Size Range	B-1 to E-4	E-4 to 7	7 to I-9	I-9 to K-10.5	K-10.5 to M-13	M-13 and larger

CROCHET HOOKS

U.S.	B-1	C-2	D-3	E-4	F-5	G-6	H-8	I-9	J-10	K-10½	N	P	Q
Metric - mm	2.25	2.75	3.25	3.5	3.75	4	5	5.5	6	6.5	9	10	15

■□□□ BEGINNER	Projects for first-time crocheters using basic stitches. Minimal shaping.
■■□□ EASY	Projects using yarn with basic stitches, repetitive stitch patterns, simple color changes, and simple shaping and finishing.
■■■□ INTERMEDIATE	Projects using a variety of techniques, such as basic lace patterns or color patterns, mid-level shaping and finishing.
■■■■ EXPERIENCED	Projects with intricate stitch patterns, techniques and dimension, such as non-repeating patterns, multi-color techniques, fine threads, small hooks, detailed shaping and refined finishing.

MARKERS

Markers are used to help distinguish the beginning of each round being worked. Place a 2" (5 cm) scrap piece of yarn before the first stitch of each round, moving marker after each round is complete.

JOINING WITH SC

When instructed to join with sc, begin with a slip knot on hook. Insert hook in stitch or space indicated, YO and pull up a loop, YO and draw through both loops on hook.

POST STITCH

Work around post of stitch indicated, inserting hook in direction of arrow (Fig. 1).

Fig. 1

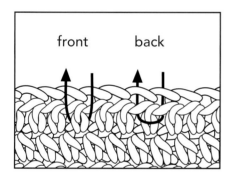

WORKING AROUND

Work in stitch or space indicated, inserting hook in direction of arrow (Fig. 2).

Fig. 2

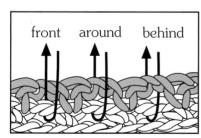

WORKING IN FRONT OR BEHIND

Work in front or behind st(s) as indicated (Fig. 3a or Fig. 3b).

Fig. 3a

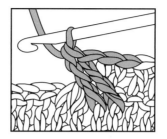

Fig. 3b

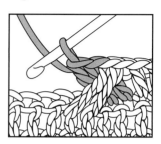

WHIPSTITCH

Place two Squares or Strips with **wrong** sides together. Beginning in center sc of first corner 3-sc group, sew through both pieces once to secure the beginning of the seam, leaving an ample yarn end to weave in later. Insert the needle from **front** to **back** through **inside** loops only of each stitch on **both** pieces (*Fig. 4*). Bring the needle around and insert it from **front** to **back** through next loops of both pieces. Continue in this manner across center sc of next corner 3-sc group, keeping the sewing yarn fairly loose.

Fig. 4

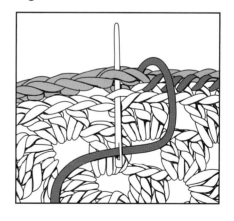

FREE LOOPS

When instructed to work in free loops of a chain, work in loop indicated by arrow (*Fig. 5*).

Fig. 5

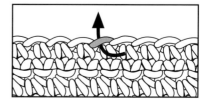

YARN INFORMATION

Each project in this leaflet was made using Bernat® Satin yarn. Any brand of Medium Weight Yarn may be used. It is best to refer to the yardage/meters when determining how many balls or skeins to purchase. Remember, to arrive at the finished size, it is the GAUGE/TENSION that is important, not the brand of yarn.
For your convenience, listed below are the specific colors used to create our photography models.

AFGHAN
#04007 Silk

BOLSTER PILLOW
Brown - #04011 Sable
Tan - #04010 Camel
Lt Green - #04320 Spring
Green - #04232 Sage
Ecru - #04007 Silk

SQUARE PILLOW
Brown - #04011 Sable
Tan - #04010 Camel
Lt Green - #04320 Spring
Green - #04232 Sage
Ecru - #04007 Silk

Production Team: Technical Editor - Lois J. Long; Editorial Writer - Susan McManus Johnson; Senior Publications Designer - Dana Vaughn; and Photo Stylist - Sondra Daniels.

We have made every effort to ensure that these instructions are accurate and complete. We cannot, however, be responsible for human error, typographical mistakes, or variations in individual work.